SUMATRAN SHADOWS

Peter Janssen

SUMATRAN SHADOWS

a family memoir

SUMATRAN SHADOWS

Copyright © 2019 by Peter Janssen

First published in 2019

Published by Peter Janssen
bkkjanssen@gmail.com

Cover illustration copyright © 2019 by Henrietta Sampson
Cover design and interior design by Henrietta Sampson,
www.bookdesignservices.com
Editing by Sean Sampson

To my mother and sister, two great ladies.

Contents

PROLOGUE

My sister and I boarded a plane at Polonia Airport, Medan, North Sumatra, on December 14, 1957, accompanied by our Dutch grandparents on a flight to nearby Singapore, leaving our parents behind at the terminal. Josie, my sister, was almost three and I was one. My American mother, Nancy Janssen, then 24, watched as her two children were flown to safety, away from the Indonesia she had come to love. December 1957 brought a dramatic end to the first four years of her marriage to my father Herbert Janssen, a fourth-generation descendent of two Dutch entrepreneurs who had played a pivotal role in transforming Medan into one of the most prosperous entrepots of the Dutch East Indies, founded on tobacco plantations and coolie labor.

"[A friend] had made a ponytail for Josie and when they finally left, she marched out to the plane with a red ribbon bouncing purposefully," my mother wrote in a diary she kept on the "expulsion." She wrote "They left and the nervous tension of the last few days began to subside. We went home." My parents stayed on in Medan for a few weeks after our hasty departure and finally flew to Singapore in early January 1958. They were among the last of some 46,000

Dutch citizens and family members forced to leave Indonesia on a month's notice by President Sukarno, Indonesia's independence hero.

The Sumatra years were to shadow the lives of my parents, whose marriage finally fell apart in 1966 in another tropical paradise in the West Indies. As a couple they were both escapists, fleeing the more ordinary, humdrum existence that beckoned in the USA, the land of my mother's birth and where they had met and become high school sweethearts. After their marriage in 1953, my parents moved to North Sumatra, Indonesia, where my father was employed as a junior manager of tobacco plantations belonging to the Senembah Company, a firm founded by Christian Janssen, his great-uncle, and listed on the Amsterdam stock exchange.

My father was the scion of two business clans started by his great grandfather Peter William Janssen I, an Amsterdam-based Dutch grain merchant of German descent, and another great-grandfather, Jacob Theodore Cremer. The latter was a brilliant manager who turned the Sumatra-based Deli Company, founded in 1869, into a household name in Holland and Sumatran tobacco leaf into the most popular wrapper leaf for cigars in Europe when cigars were still all the rage and before the invention of the cigarette popularized smoking. These two families made their fortunes off the tobacco trade, establishing themselves among the 'Indies riche,' the class of Dutch nouveaux riches of the Dutch East Indies.

My mother was the offspring of an upper-middle-class American family steeped in Christian Science, an offbeat Protestant denomination started by Mary Baker Eddy in 1875. The group is best known for its prohibition against visiting doctors and using medicine, preaching that prayer and the proper understanding of the Bible can induce self-healing. This religion brought my parents together, as a desire to provide my father with a Christian Science environment after the Janssen family had spent three years in Japanese concentration camps in Indonesia during World War II, was the reason he was sent to the USA to attend a Christian Science high school, where my parents met.

After their marriage, they moved to North Sumatra, living there between 1953 and 1957, and where my sister Josie Janssen was born on April 29, 1955. I (Peter William Janssen III, better known by my nickname PayVay, or P.W.) was born in Hilversum, the Netherlands, on November 30, 1956, but returned to North Sumatra for the first year of my life. It proved to be a short stay for me.

Our family was forced to flee along with some 46,000 other Dutch people in December 1957, on the abrupt orders of Indonesia's president. Sukarno, annoyed with the Netherlands' refusal to include West New Guinea as a sovereign state under independent Indonesia, ordered the lingering Dutch families to leave within a month. All Dutch-owned businesses were nationalized. It was an ignoble end to 350 years of often brutal Dutch colonialism in the Dutch East Indies.

It was also the end of my father's aspirations to rise in the family-run Senembah Company, which, according to company records, had designated him as the future director of the tobacco plantation operations. My father's career and life floundered because of his lack of higher education and, perhaps, direction and ambition, in the aftermath of the Sumatra expulsion. The marriage ended about ten years later on the island of Grenada, in the West Indies, where our family had migrated in the footsteps of my grandfather Peter

William Janssen II, and his wife Lutske Janssen ("Pooh" to my sister and me).

As a child I grew up hearing tales of Sumatra and as an adult had urged my mother to write a memoir about her years there, and perhaps the less exotic years in Grenada. She experienced two dramatic departures in her life, first from North Sumatra, as an evacuee from Sukarno's wrath, and later from Grenada, fleeing a failed marriage and moving back to the United States, where my sister and I accompanied her, once again getting on a plane that would leave part of our lives behind.

Our lives in the USA were ordinary. My mother went back to Sarah Lawrence college and became a music teacher at Derryfield, a college preparatory high school in Manchester, New Hampshire, where she eventually fell in love with the French teacher, Philip Currier, and remarried. Their union has been a happy one and a great blessing for my mother, who always had a romantic streak.

My mother never did get around to writing her memoir, and then after she started to suffer from dementia in her early 80s, I took up the task myself, turning it into more of a family memoir. As a journalist who has spent his career in Southeast Asia, including a stint in Indonesia between 2001 and 2004, I felt prepared for the task, at least in compiling the history and facts.

Although I have always loved my mother deeply and thank her for instilling in me an appreciation for classical music, Asian cuisine, travel, reading and an aspiration to follow her fine sense of fairness in dealing with fellow human beings, it is difficult to capture someone's personality and the inner workings of a life. Why, for instance, was my mother attracted to an odd Dutchman and an exotic life in the Orient when she was a young American woman? Why did she later agree to accompany her husband to Grenada, a tiny island in the Caribbean where the main source of entertainment was watching the sun set while drinking rum (especially, since as a practicing Christian Scientist, she couldn't partake)? Did she regret any of her youthful decisions? When friends and relatives express their sympathies for my mother's early misfortunes and personal traumas, my only response is, "At least it was interesting."

CHAPTER 1

TEMPO DULU

When I was a teenager my mother, then the music teacher at the high school my sister and I were attending in Manchester, New Hampshire, would occasionally entertain her colleagues and friends with a dinner party. In the summer months, there were barbeques at our 200-year-old rented house out in "the woods" on Stowell Road, but during the cold winter months she would often lay out a fiery *rijst tafel*, a Dutch phrase which translates literally as "rice table." *Rijst tafel* was a term coined in the East Indies, conjuring up leisurely days of tropical bounty in the former Dutch colony of Indonesia.

A good *rijst tafel* is a smorgasbord of Indonesian and sometimes Western dishes, with a mountain of saffron rice at its center, surrounded by a massive assortment of curries, meats, condiments, canned goods and desserts. My mother's *rijst tafels* were more modest affairs, typically comprising a *nasi goreng* (fried rice), chicken curry, *sapi rendang* (beef curry), chicken satay and *gado gado* (mixed vegetables with peanut sauce). These repasts were my loving introduction to Asian cuisine and always succeeded in wowing our American guests. My mother would then regale the table with tales of Sumatra, Indonesia, where she spent the first four years of her marriage to my father, Herbert Janssen.

Those exotic stories of Indonesia, where I spent the first, unremembered year of my life, always left me a bit in awe of my mother's past life in the Orient and stirred a yearning in my own breast to repeat her experiences in some fashion. When I graduated from St. John's College, a liberal arts institution that specializes in the history of Western thought (not the best preparation for my adult life in the East), I managed to get on a study program at the Chinese University of Hong Kong. That was my return ticket to Asia. After a year in Hong Kong, studying Mandarin in the then-British colony where the locals all spoke Cantonese (the predominant dialect of Guangdong

Family home in Bedford, New Hampshire, where my mother used to cook spicey Indonesian cuisine during the cold winter months.
Photo credit: Peter Janssen

province in southern China), I moved to Bangkok, Thailand, in 1980 and began a lifetime career in journalism in Southeast Asia.

Between 2001 and 2004, I transferred from Bangkok to Jakarta, Indonesia, where I was bureau chief for Deutsche Presse-Agentur (the German Press Agency dpa) and a stringer for Newsweek magazine. I had intended it to be a journey of *tempo dulu*, the Indonesian term for "time past," or "nostalgia." Unfortunately, for me it turned into a very busy period news-wise what with US President George W. Bush's invasion of Afghanistan and the "war on terror," essentially a war on "Muslim terror" (Indonesia is the world's largest Muslim-majority nation), the Bali bombing in 2002 and thereafter the Marriott Hotel bombing in Jakarta in 2004. I didn't have as much time as I had hoped for exploring my family's history in North Sumatra, which is far from Jakarta, Indonesia's capital on the island of Java.

I did manage to arrange one excursion in 2003 with my American family to Medan, North Sumatra's capital, where my mother and father had lived together between 1953 and 1957. Our group comprised my mother, Nancy Janssen-Currier, my stepfather Philip Currier, my sister Josie Janssen and her two children Tyrone and Molly, my Thai-Chinese wife Suwannee and our kids Sarah and Herbert. We hired a minibus, got a guide and visited a tobacco factory near Medan which might have been one my father worked in (but probably wasn't), the hospital where my sister was born in 1955, and the Tip Top restaurant in Medan which my mother frequented on weekends during her shopping trips to town, and remains there today still serving my mother's favorite Café Vienna.

The house where we lived in Batang Kuis, North Sumatra, during my parents' four years there, rediscovered during a family visit to Sumatra in 2003. Photo Credit: Peter Janssen

While tootling around the outskirts of Medan in our rented minibus, my mother said, "Please stop. That is our old home." It was in Batang Kuis district, where my father had been stationed as a junior manager of the Senembah Company, one of the largest Dutch tobacco companies, set up in the early 1890s by Christian Janssen, my great-great uncle. We got out of our minibus and crowded on to the front veranda of the bungalow, solidly built on a foundation of massive stone blocks.

An elderly Indonesian woman opened the door and looked at this crowd of *bule* (white people) with astonishment. Our guide explained that we were on a *tempo dulu* tour and her house appeared to be where we had lived five decades ago. The woman, who turned out to be the wife of an Indonesian doctor, graciously permitted our troop to enter.

"That was your room," my mother said to my sister and me. "This was where Herb and I slept." Then a quick visit to the outdoor kitchen and the *mandi*, or toilet, where my mother had bravely slapped scorpions and centipedes dead with her flip-flops on midnight visits to the loo.

My mother met my father in St. Louis, Missouri, USA. They were both attending the Principia, a preparatory high school, a sheltered privately-run institution under the umbrella of the Christian Science Church, a Protestant offshoot sect started by Mary Baker Eddy, author of *Science and Health and Key to the Scriptures*. Christian Scientists believe in the power of self-healing (man is the image and likeness of God so he is perfect and that perfection must be manifested in faith) and don't believe in going to doctors, taking medicine, smoking, drinking alcohol or any other activities that might be deemed "fun" or "putting graven images before God."

Henriette Jetske Cremer, my father's mother (i.e. my Dutch grandmother) was a Christian Scientist too. How she became a Christian Scientist in Holland is a bit of a family mystery, although the sect was relatively popular at the time in Holland and Britain. It is possible that her own grandmother, Annie Hermine Hogan (1854-1924), was introduced to the unusual American sect while her husband and one of my great-great grandfathers, Jacob Theodore Cremer (1847-1923), was posted to Washington D.C. as Dutch Ambassador from 1918 to 1919. No one really knows who converted Granny but converted she was and the religion was much on her mind in 1945 when the remnants of the battered Janssen clan gathered at the luxurious Raffles Hotel in Singapore to lick their wounds.

My father, my grandfather—Peter William Janssen II, my granny—Jetske, and my father's sister Mienske and his older brother August all spent the war years (1942 to 1945) in Japanese concentration camps in Indonesia. A second sister, Elizabeth, my father's favorite sibling, died in the camps, probably of dysentery, although it could have been dengue, malaria or cholera. Some members of the Janssen family blamed Jetske for Elizabeth's death, claiming she refused to give her even the scarce medicines available in the camps because of her Christian Science beliefs. This family rumor is impossible to confirm or disprove. What is known is that once they got out of the camps and were safely ensconced in the Raffles Hotel in nearby Singapore, granny still believed in the religion and decided that what her traumatized offspring needed was a good Christian Science environment and education.

"Today is Elizabeth's birthday," my father wrote on November 30, 1945, in a diary he kept in Singapore. "Nobody talks about her. That makes it really hard," he said of his beloved sister. "I am glad we are all with the Science. My grief is more bearable for me because of Science." He was 15 years old. Dad would turn out to be lousy Christian Scientist—he was an avid smoker and dedicated drinker—in the long run, but in the short run Christian Science was his ticket to the USA where he would eventually meet my mother. The Janssen clan (granny, August, Mienske and Herbert) took a ship from Singapore to the USA, arriving in New York on February 24, 1946. Herbert was accepted in the Principia High School and August and Mienske made it into Principia College, a sister institution located nearby in Elsa Bluffs, Illinois.

My mother attended Principia High School between 1947 and 1950. Her mother and father were both Christian Scientists and they too were drawn into the religion by strong-willed grandmothers. My mother's grandmother was Gertrude Rhiner Taylor, a descendent of German immigrants, who married John Taylor, founder of the John Taylor Dry Goods Company in Kansas City. Family rumor has it that Gertrude had started out at the John Taylor Dry Goods store as a salesclerk and worked her way up to be the wife of the boss. Given her humble origins, Grandma Gertrude was perhaps never fully accepted among the social elite in Short Hills, New Jersey, an upscale suburb of New York City. She was attracted to Christian Science after her husband contracted an incurable disease. He died at the age of 60, leaving a considerable fortune to his offspring and wife.

Mom's mother, Ruth Taylor DeGarmo (my American grandmother), and her father George DeGarmo (my

American grandfather), were devout Christian Scientists. Grandfather George was introduced to the religion by his mother Sidney Wilson, originally a Quaker who was drawn to Christian Science after losing her first son, a pilot, in World War I. George would also join up for World War I, lying about his age in order to get in. He was thereafter too old to sign up in World War II for active duty but joined the USAAF anyway and played a pivotal role in introducing aerial photography to the service, an innovation that did much to improve reconnaissance and aerial bombings. He spent much of the war in the South Pacific. After the war, they were all shipped off to Christian Science schools, much like the Janssens.

BOY MEETS GIRL

My parents "fell in love" in the Principia. The relationship was initiated by my father, in the winter of 1948. "We went to an ice-skating event and we got back on the bus which we had to stand on, holding straps, and Herbert just got right up behind me and I thought, 'Oh my gosh! What is this about?'" my mother recalled. "But I must have responded. And somewhere in the next two weeks or so, I just went gaga for him."

They were not a likely couple. Dad was short for his age, had freckles and curly red hair, was a poor student and was always getting into trouble with the school authorities. Mom was a beauty, a brunette, petite, a straight A student, a good Christian Scientist and a talented pianist. In my dad's favor was his horrendous experience in the Japanese concentration camps and a similarly terrible childhood

My father and mother (the escapists).

in Holland, perfect fodder for my mother's great capacity for sympathy. "He loved his sister," my mother told me, decades later after her marriage to my father had fallen apart on another island on the other side of the world. "Elizabeth was the person he loved the most and so he transferred his love from Elizabeth on to me, his feeling of need." As for her feelings for him, she recalled, "He was interesting. He was also very needy, and he was very lost."

My father apparently played on my mother's sympathies, wooing her with horror stories of his teenage years behind barbed wire in Java and of his frigid upbringing under a series of governesses in Holland. One German nanny attained family legend status for her sadistic streak, or perhaps it was just good Prussian child-rearing techniques. Schwester Lizel, from Bavaria, would hold the children under water in the bathtub if they misbehaved or hose them off naked outside with freezing water in the middle of the Dutch winter. She once forced dad's brother August to eat a piece of liver he had surreptitiously slipped behind a radiator to avoid eating two days previously. The parents were strangely absent from the picture, or silently approved of the discipline.

"When I really fell in love with him was when he described to me his mother's necklace," my mother said of my father's courtship. "We were at a concert and I had a pearl necklace, and Herb said to me that when he was a child his mother had a very long pearl necklace and when she came to kiss him good night he would open his mouth and take all the pearls in so she couldn't leave. That's when I realized how neglected he had been as a child and I felt so badly for him. So my first instinct to love him was out of sympathy," my mother said in an interview with Molly Saldo, my niece, for one of her high school writing projects.

They became "sweethearts" in 1949-1950, apparently too overtly for the puritanical headmaster of Principia, who called Mom in for a lecture. "The headmaster said, 'You know, I don't like this display of affection, and Herbert is so in love with you that this is not good, and this is not a good combination,'" Mom recalled. "But I didn't pay any attention. As soon as he said that I liked Herb even more," said my Mom, the rebel.

Mom also became a rule breaker. Herbert and Nancy would go up to Principia College on weekends to visit Trudie (Mom's elder sister) and August (Dad's elder brother) to attend dances there. Principia College is perched above the Mississippi River. "There was a very beautiful pathway along the Mississippi River and we went out in the moonlight and walked along it. Of course, we were doing a bad thing, because we weren't supposed to have left the dance hall, but Herbert didn't care about regulations. He thought it was all funny, and by comparison with his life in the concentration camps it was a joke."

Mom would not go on to Principia College after finishing Principia High School, in part because of the worries of her mother. Grandmother Ruth, a woman of strong convictions, was sure that if Mom and Trude were in the same school they would fall in love with the same man, and Mom would triumph. "She thought I was doomed to be a licentious person, a Jezebel," Mom said of her mother. This turned out to be a plus because it meant she was not forced to go to Principia College. Instead she went to Sarah Lawrence, an all-female liberal arts college in Bronxville, New York.

"I loved Sarah Lawrence," Mom recalled of her college years in the early 1950s. "Girls wore pants and Bermuda shorts and they smoked in class. My first roommate was strange and distant. She went to New York most days and was having an affair with both her piano teacher and his wife. This was all new stuff for me." Her housemother was a black woman whose father was a "big shot" in New York. "She was wonderful, and I loved her," Mom said.

But things were not going well on the love front that first year at Sarah Lawrence. In 1950, Herbert returned to Holland and then to Sumatra, to join the family business of running tobacco and rubber plantations and exporting the commodities to the Netherlands. At this stage he also decided to break up with mother, apparently because he was having an affair with "an older woman."

"I was heart-broken because I was not the sort of person to just have a casual boyfriend and I was so into the love thing, the romantic nonsense," Mom said. Dad was no romantic. "Not a bit, but he did love me in his own way," she said. And he came back, to work in Connecticut, USA, where Granny Jetske's brother Theodore Cremer had opened a business importing tobacco from Sumatra to make small, factory-rolled cigars for the American market. With the "older woman" apparently no longer in the picture, Dad decided to resume the relationship with Mom, commuting to New York to see her over weekends.

Opa, which is what my sister and I called my Dutch Grandfather—Peter William Janssen II—was always a big supporter of my mother. "His father was definitely pushing the whole idea as a good match, thinking that I would be able to change Herb's wild side and make him into a good, respectable person, which I never could. But Papa was extremely nice to me and extremely eager for Herbert to continue on with the relationship."

Opa himself had a bit of a "wild side," and a "romantic" bent. In his youth in Holland, as an heir to the Janssen tobacco fortunes, he was seen as one of the most eligible bachelors in the Netherlands—tall, handsome and rich. When a teenager, his mother hired a prostitute to introduce him to sex, and, apparently, he enjoyed the lesson. He had had many affairs by the time his own father August Janssen decided it was time he settled down to a good business marriage with Jetske, an heir in her own right to the massive

Cremer fortunes, which were intimately interlinked with the Janssen legacy in Sumatra. The marriage was doomed. By 1952, Opa had divorced Jetske and married his long-time girlfriend Lutske Nicolai, whom he had met in Sumatra. Opa had gone to see the Hollywood movie Gigi—about a handsome, rich dude who ends up marrying his designated mistress—16 times.

Ruth and George DeGarmo were less enthusiastic about the Herbert-Nancy relationship, which had turned more "intimate" by 1952. "My parents were worried we were going to have a baby before marriage since he's visiting me and I'm visiting him all the time, so it was decided, probably by his father and Jetske, that we would get married before he got sent off to Indonesia and I would follow behind," Mom said of the marriage preparations. They tied the knot on May 19, 1953, in a modest ceremony held at the DeGarmo home in Red Bank, New Jersey. Mom had to leave her beloved Sarah Lawrence College in the middle of her Junior year. "The dean of the college told me, 'You'll be back.'" That proved prophetic.

OFF TO THE ORIENT

After the wedding, Herb and Nancy flew to Holland, for two weeks of fun before heading to Sumatra. Opa and Lutske took them to Paris, where Mom saw her first cabaret show, featuring a beautiful dancer who took off a wig at the end of the performance, revealing his true identity. Mom was impressed.

The relationship between Dad and his stepmother Lutske (whom we always called Pooh, after Winnie the Pooh...

a nickname Josie bequeathed on her) was often strained. Opa had divorced Granny and married Lutske in 1952, shortly before my parents' wedding. Lutske was a powerhouse of a woman, beautiful and bossy. "Sometimes they got into terrible arguments if she was too domineering, but, on the whole, he got along with Lutske," Mom said of the relationship between Lutske and Herb. "Lutske and Papa wanted me to be the peace-maker among all of them, a job I took on without any hesitation."

After two weeks in Europe, Herb and Nancy took a ship from southern Spain to Singapore, passing through the Suez Canal. Herbert spent a few days in Singapore, staying at the Raffles Hotel, of course, before travelling on to Medan, to get back to work before his visa expired. Mom stayed at Raffles for two or three weeks, awaiting her own visa to Indonesia. Two Canadian ladies at the hotel, a lesbian couple according to my mother, took her under their wing on their visits to the botanical garden, the zoo and museums. The visa was finally approved, and Mom took a small plane to Penang, Malaysia, then caught an even smaller plane to Medan, which would be her home for the next four and a half years.

Medan, dubbed the "Paris of Sumatra" by the Dutch, was a fairly cosmopolitan enclave of money-minded foreigners in 1953. It was a city based on commerce, founded on the logistical requirements of the first tobacco plantation established in the Deli district by a Dutch pioneer, Jacob Nienhuys, and financed by my great-great grandfather, Peter Wilhelm Janssen, a German-born grain merchant based in Amsterdam. Medan was transformed from a logistics base on the Babura River into a thriving metropolis thanks, in part, to the efforts of another great-great grandfather,

Jacob Theodore Cremer, who headed the Deli Maatschappij (Company) between 1871 and 1882, building it into one of the most profitable operations in Indonesia and the first Sumatra-based company to get listed on the Amsterdam Stock Exchange. That achievement was based on the sweat of first Chinese and then Javanese "coolies," who slaved away on the tobacco plantations that initially made Medan a commercial success story.

My mother, a 20-year-old newly married woman, was thrown into this Dutch world without a great deal of academic preparation. She had majored in music at Sarah Lawrence, but took one course in Asian studies in her junior year when it became clear that she would be heading for the Orient in the near future. She had read little of Indonesia and only knew of the family history there through the anecdotes of the Janssen family, who tended to embellish their enlightened role in the former colony. At that time, the Janssens and Cremers were in fact holding onto the family fortunes by their fingertips.

The Janssen family had stayed in Indonesia during World War II, spending three years in Japanese concentration camps. Theo Cremer, the brother of Jetske, had won a coin flip with my grandfather before the war and got on a steamer for the USA with the last huge shipment of Sumatran tobacco. He made a small fortune off its sale in the tobacco-deprived US market, which he then invested in a new "shade grown" tobacco operation in Connecticut. Meanwhile, in Indonesia, the Janssens rotted away in the concentration camps.

At the end of the war, Indonesia declared independence, which the Dutch were forced to concede after some bloody fighting with the local militias that had been cultivated during the Japanese occupation under the leadership of Sukarno, who would later become the first President of Indonesia (1949-1967). The post-World War II years were nasty times in Indonesia, with atrocities committed on both sides. Tensions between Sukarno and the Dutch government remained high, because while ceding Indonesia its independence in 1949, Holland refused to include the huge territory of West Papua in the equation, claiming with some justification, that Papua was a separate country by history, language and ethnicity and so deserved its own independence at an unspecified date in the future. Sukarno thought otherwise, but an uneasy truce was declared with the 200,000 Dutch residents of Indonesia who were allowed to stay on in the former colony, conducting business as usual.

Into this complex whirlwind of post-colonial struggles drifted my mother, an idealistic young American woman with liberal notions on racial equality and social justice, not to mention a firm believer in Christian Science which disapproved of smoking and alcohol consumption—the main pastimes of the expatriates stationed in North Sumatra. "I didn't know anything about Indonesia, but I was very excited to be there," Mom recalled. She had to start studying both Dutch and Indonesian to communicate with the locals, i.e. the Dutch community, most of whom were a lot older than her, and the Indonesians, primarily the three or four household servants that came with each plantation bungalow. Mom, always a good student, had plenty of time to study and was soon proficient in both languages. "A musical background was helpful in studying languages," she noted. It's been my own experience that language study is facilitated by two things—a musical ear and a brilliant memory; Mom had both.

My father and mother lived privileged lives in North Sumatra. Herbert was the son of Peter W. Janssen II, great-grandson of the Peter W. Janssen I who had invested in the first tobacco plantation in Deli District and was a founder of the Deli Company in 1868. His son Christian Janssen had started the Senembah Company, which became the second-largest tobacco operation in North Sumatra after only the Deli Company. When my mother arrived in Medan in 1953, my grandfather was chairman of the Senembah Company and my father was a junior manager learning the ropes with aspirations of rising in the corporate ranks. As my father was the son of the chairman, my parents enjoyed certain special privileges.

"For the first few weeks, we lived in one of the executive houses. It was very stylish and comfortable," Mom said of her introduction to Medan. "And then we were put out after we had acclimatized a bit, and that's when I started collecting dogs." My mother would end up with three stray dogs, named Peter, Theo and Polo, who would accompany her on her morning strolls around the tobacco plantations. "Every day I would go walking and they would come walking with me and leap into the gullies along the road and chase after things and I would go screaming after them. They were very disobedient. The local people thought it was very strange that I would get up and put on my short pants, but all they would say is, *Pergi mana Ma'am?* (Where are you going, Ma'am?) and I would say *Jalan, jalan,* (I'm walking). But the dogs kept them from being too curious. Indonesians do not like dogs."

LIFE ON THE PLANTATION

From 1950 to 1957, the Janssen-Cremer fortunes were on an upswing. My mother would arrive just in time to experience four years of renewed Dutch optimism about their future in Indonesia. After being shut down during World War II and having much of their tobacco plantation lands used for agriculture to feed the local population, the Deli and Senembah companies enjoyed a revival in the early 1950s, fueled by growing demand for rubber because of the Korean war (1950-1953) and healthy exports of tobacco and palm oil to Europe and the USA.

The renewed fortunes gave rise to hopes that the boom days were back, especially for my father, Herbert, who had foregone college in the US to join the family-run Senembah Company. Nepotism was the norm in those days. According to Senembah Company records, seen by my step-uncle Wouter Nicolai when he was working as a World Bank consultant in the 1980s, Herbert was being groomed to take over the tobacco side of the plantation business, while Wouter, his step-brother, was in line to manage the company's palm oil and rubber plantation. Neither job would materialize.

While my father struggled to secure his place in the Senembah Company, my mother was walking her dogs, learning Indonesian and Dutch, and, eventually, having babies. Her elder sister, Trude, visited in December 1954, staying for the holiday season. Trude wrote letters back to her parents that provide a small glimpse of my parents' lifestyle. "The Dutch are a bit dull socially, at least the majority of the ones who come out to these plantations. The life, however, on the estates is much more comfortable and entertaining than I had pictured it," she wrote in a letter dated December 10, 1954.

Trude spent the holidays in Medan, travelling up to the nearby hill station in Brastagi to celebrate Christmas Day. Her letters suggest that a good time was had by all. "I nearly fell off my mount laughing at Herb the morning we went riding. He drew a jug [loser] and would disappear up every driveway we passed," she wrote. And on New Year's Eve, she wrote "Last night we had two bachelors to dinner. We used French at dinner since it was the only language that none of us knew enough about to say anything in. Herb always recites stanzas of the French national anthem with great speed when he's called upon to use this language, which gets a big laugh from all quarters." Trude departed

My father (hamming it up for the camera), mother and Dutch friend in a tobacco field, North Sumatra.

on January 10, 1955, leaving my mother to prepare for the birth of her first child.

Josie, my sister, was born on April 29, 1955, in the Tand-jong Morawa Hospital, part of the Tandjong Morawa complex that housed the headquarters of the Senembah Company. As a practicing Christian Scientist, Mom was opposed to going to a hospital even for something as poten-tially dangerous as a birth in the tropics. After agreeing to go, she made a big point out of taking as little medicine as possible. Josie's birth was without difficulties. "After the birth, I was so elated and grateful—I was also a little proud and 'I told you so' with all the good ladies who visited me and I made no secret of the fact that I had not had com-plications or trouble," Mom wrote in a letter to her parents on May 15, 1955.

But there were breast-feeding complications when she was at home, and more Christian Science angst. She got an infection and fever from over-milking (my Mom, the over-achiever). "Well, the result was I came [to hospital] ... it has involved regular helpings of sulphur tablets. I pro-tested over these, but I had put myself back here and the doctor has foregone the apparently usual packs, plasters, shots, etc ... I felt very low about the whole thing," she wrote. "Hope you will understand the weaknesses of your wayward daughter." Wayward, indeed.

I arrived a year-and-a-half later and was two weeks late at that. Instead of Medan, I was born in Hilversum, Hol-land, at the tail end of a four-month period my parents and sister Josie spent in Denmark, living with a young Danish couple, Ian and Christin Kjerr. The Senembah Company was looking into setting up a joint venture with the Kjerr's family company, in an attempt to dilute its Dutch holdings in case of growing anti-Dutch sentiments in Indonesia. The Danish interlude provided a good excuse to stay in Europe for my delivery on November 30, 1956. I was named Peter William Janssen, after my grandfather and his grandfather (a Dutch tradition) but my mother always called me PW, or Pay Vay, which is the Dutch pronunciation of P and W.

"PW is two pounds heavier than Josie, but the doctors carefully and slowly massaged him into this world without a break or stitch," my mother wrote in her diary on December 2, 1956. "What a thrill to see PW's small head and then whole self—comic in his grief and his greasy coating—purple tinted from his efforts and furious to be dislocated. A son is born—fulfillment of the Chinese prophesy—first the flower and then the fruit." As it turned out, my sister, who became a successful social worker in Massachusetts, USA, undoubtedly led a more fruitful life than I have.

My mother was always fair, when it came to her love of my sister and me. On December 4, 1956, she wrote: "Have been trying to decide how my present respective love for Jos and PW differs. Now that she is so companionable and so clearly personal in her small developed self, I love Josie with an intimacy and intensity that borders on adoration and self-conceit. With this birth—especially easy but less spectacular in the beginning—I have felt more humility and consequently am more ready to go beyond the human wonder. My love for PW is close to all manifestations of mother love in its first form which is instinct. The one motive feeling is protection and care without any expectation of shared affection. Well-being is enough reward. At this moment, mother love is in its most primitive form—held in common with all creatures—animal and human."

WHAT AM I DOING HERE?

The family flew back to Sumatra in February 1957, for what would turn out to be an eventful year for the Janssens and 46,000 other Dutch people living in Indonesia. My father's prospects in the Senembah Company were on the rise, but on the condition that he stayed in Indonesia. Before departing for Sumatra, he had a talk with Koos Schoon, the general manager of Senembah. "Herb's own talk with him went well, mainly because he prefaced all remarks with the idea that he is more interested in Indonesia than Holland. Koos responded like a delighted child with a rush of ideas to fill in Herb's training."

Schoon was generally despised by my parents and seen as the main barrier to my father's advancement, at least in my mother's eyes. There was a small victory over Schoon at a party hosted by the Sultan of Medan for Theo Cremer, my father's uncle and the descendent of Jacob Theodore Cremer who started the Deli Company and rose to be minister of the colonies in the Netherlands. My mother described the event in her dairy on February 18, 1957, which gives a nice taste of what her social life was like in Medan.

"The Sultan's party for Uncle Theo may bring up more conclusions than merely our childish sense of victory over Koos. We did look nice. Herb was surprisingly neat in his new wonder suit and even fastened the button under his tie. Probably my dress should be altered so it doesn't show so much bosom but at least last week there was some bosom to see before the feeding time. The Sultan clung with hope to Uncle Theo. Perhaps Uncle Theo preferred his recognizable intentions to any vague approaches from the others. They reminded me of schoolgirls attracting attention at a stag dance.

"As usual, Koos was dressed in a fashion which was immaculate but outdated and made him look 10 years older. While Herb was talking with Uncle Theo, Koos tried several times to join in—each time was rebuffed by Uncle Theo who conscientiously ignored him. In a detached way he was nice about Herb—asked when he would be given a good position which he thought he deserved. He managed to say that Herb had no competition here."

My father's prospects at the Senembah Company may have been looking up, but those of the company in Indonesia were getting bleaker. Sukarno, Indonesia's charismatic first post-independence president, was turning up his

My mother and her best friend, Peggy Liau, a Sino-Indonesian married to the CFO of the Senembah Company.

anti-Dutch rhetoric in 1957 over the New Guinea conflict and threatening to kick all the Dutch "colonialists" out and confiscate their property. The prosperous Dutch-owned tobacco, rubber and palm oil plantations in North Sumatra were an obvious target.

As the anti-Dutch protests gathered steam in Jakarta, the capital, my mother started to detect a change in her good friend Peggy Liau, an Indonesian-Chinese woman married to the chief financial officer at Senembah Company. My mother's close friendship with Peggy, who had three children, ran counter to the social norms in Dutch plantation society but never bothered my mother. She did, however, in May 1957, detect a change in the Liaus' attitude towards the Dutch. "Friendly to both Europeans and Asians, I felt for the first time that Peggy was loosening her bond to Europeans and leaning towards her own race more decidedly than before," Nancy wrote in her diary on May 26, 1957. "This may be a strong Chinese instinct to pick the winning side. This may be a political barometer since they're usually ready for something before it happens." Something was, indeed, about to happen.

With political tensions on the rise, and after four years in Sumatra where she had been exposed to both Dutch and Indonesian cultures, far away from her protected Christian-Science world on the East Coast of the USA, my mother was turning increasingly reflective and introspective about her own life choices. In a letter to the alumni magazine of Sarah Lawrence College, which was never sent or published, she wrote of the Indonesian political situation: "I wouldn't dare to discuss Indonesian politics as such. In most countries you can study the politics systematically and begin to form judgements. Here we are in the middle of a revolutionary process and cannot be definite about many facts. The prolonged sense of rising and receding crisis—surrounded by a maximum of confusion and a burlesque of our sound rational ways drives many a Westerner back to where he came from."

But the hurly-burly of Indonesian independence politics, did not seem particularly intimidating to my mother. "How came I to be so thoroughly happy in surroundings which at the least exasperate the majority of Westerners? I am not only happy, I am actually in harmony with something here, something vital to me even if I cannot find words to describe it … It has to do with an intrinsic goodness peculiar to what I think of when I refer to the lasting Indonesia—it is a truth beyond all the surface layers of truth." My mother, at that time, had started teaching young Indonesian ladies ballet and modern dance. She appeared to be more taken with her Indonesian pupils than her Dutch companions. "By nature, they are eager, informal, willing, relaxed in their own group to being totally without inhibitions—shy with strangers but lenient with each other. In contrast, the average Dutchman is reserved, formal, highly sceptic, respectful of learning but difficult to convince that learning does exist outside Holland … They mostly feel superior and will consent to like you on the basis that you are not so bad for an American."

And what exactly was a young, liberal American woman doing in North Sumatra anyway? There was a bit of escapism lurking in Nancy Janssen and my father. In her never published alumni letter she wrote: "My own personal question is—what am I doing here? Technically, I am following my husband around but together we prefer to work here. We are hopeful for modern Indonesians because of this ancient something which could put some reality into our highest, most advanced Western ideals. On the other hand, we are only deceiving ourselves by fleeing to an ancient culture from a modern one where we feel strangely untouched by Western ambition. Are the things I turn to here, the ones which contradict the evils of my own culture and am I seeking to escape those rather than challenge what I can't accept? These are things I have to ask myself."

CHAPTER 2

END OF AN ERA

"Indonesia gives you a rare sense of tranquility—an absurd conviction that everything else must be an illusion. You look across the lazy sun-lighted stretches to the abrupt mountains and are convinced there is no beyond. The sky is big from horizon to horizon and close, so close you can feel it brush your arm with a soft touch. Until you want to get out. Then the mountains are enormous and the sky is sitting on your back."

Nancy Janssen's diary entry, December 16, 1957.

The expulsion order for some 46,000 Dutch people from Indonesia at the tail-end of 1957 came as a shock to most. The new anti-Dutch campaign began typically enough for such demonstrations, which were common occurrences in post-independence Indonesia. In Java, the most populous island of the vast archipelago, students painted slogans on public buildings and Dutch-owned houses and cars, "Go home, you Dutch dogs," and "Free Irian Barat from

My father (center) with Ietje (wife of the boss) and my mother
at the Senembah Company bar. Uncle Wouter is the tall guy
crouching on the left.

imperialism," a reference to Dutch New Guinea. Mistakes
were made. In Jakarta they put their artwork on the Bank
Indonesia headquarters, not realizing it belonged to the
independent Indonesian government. When the error was
pointed out, the students added a tag line, *Minta ampun*,
or "Please forgive."

In Medan, the capital of North Sumatra, militant students
barged into the posh Hotel Astori and splashed anti-Dutch
slogans on the doors of two rooms that happened to be
occupied by the Indonesian chief of immigration and an
American professor teaching at Batak University. The goofs
caused chuckles at the Societeit (Social Club) and Tip Top
Restaurant, two popular expatriate hangouts in Medan,
a city founded on tobacco profits and "coolie" sweat. Soon
the jokes would end when it became clear that the Indonesian government was deadly serious about the expulsion. By
March 1958, the last Dutch citizen had officially departed,

with an estimated 2,600 fleeing from North Sumatra. A few hardy souls stayed on as consultants, but most of these would also leave when the government insisted that they take Indonesian nationality if they wished to remain.

The exodus included Herbert Janssen and Nancy DeGarmo, my parents, who spent the first phase of their marriage in North Sumatra from 1953 to 1957, witnessing the death throes of 340 years of Dutch dominance in Indonesia. It was also an abrupt end to almost a century of the Janssen family's involvement in the tobacco business in Sumatra.

I had often encouraged my mother to write a memoir of her Sumatra experience but there was never enough time. When her memory began to fade in her 80's, I decided to take up the task. My mother vaguely recalled having kept a diary of her Sumatra years but had lost it somewhere in the comfortable, cluttered 200-year-old house she now shared with her second husband, Philip Currier, in New Hampshire, USA. On a visit home in March 2015, I asked my mother to track down a novel for me in their extensive library that meanders across stairwells and bedroom walls. She returned ten minutes later saying, "Look what I found. My Sumatra diary, and it covers the evacuation period." It was the last day of my vacation in the United States, before returning to my own cluttered, book-filled home in Bangkok, Thailand. I had been anguishing over how I could possibly compile a family memoir with so few recorded memories. The diary was written in 1957-58, when my mother was 25 years old.

"I was never more than an observer in their lives. It was one of those semi-accidental things when you're momentarily drawn out of your own orbit into someone else's world. People stayed at home and talked about the world and they meant the globe. Now I know how complex the world really is, how much a composite it is, made up of a multiple of smaller worlds, some intermeshed and some torn totally apart."

Diary entry, January 3, 1958.

The Cremer and Janssen families made their fortunes in Sumatra, where my great-great grandfather Peter Wilhelm Janssen I invested in a risky tobacco venture in 1867, with a Dutch entrepreneur named Jacob Nienhuys. On November 1, 1869, the two men set up the Deli Company, the first Dutch East Indies-based company listed on the Amsterdam stock market, with the royally connected Dutch Trading Company holding 50 percent of the shares. Jacob Theodore Cremer was hired as the company's managing director in 1871, and swiftly turned it into a commercial success. The company planted, cured and shipped abroad Deli wrapper, the outer leaf of a hand-rolled cigar, which became world-famed for its good flavor and durability.

After decades of shared business dealings in tobacco, rubber and palm oil, the Cremer and Janssen families forged blood ties in 1924 when Henriette Jetske Cremer, my Dutch grandmother, married Peter William Janssen II, my Dutch grandfather. It was seen as a "business marriage," and doomed to end in divorce.

Granny was a delicate creature, born into the unreal world of the nouveaux riches, who grew up with a bevy of servants to comb her hair and dress her up like a little princess. At the age of 80, when I visited her once in Colorado, USA, she was very pleased with herself for having learned how to make a soft-boiled egg. The one she made for me still looked like an embryo, but I ate it, anyway. How she survived the Japanese concentration camps from 1942 to 1945, and at least one special detention by the Japanese police in which she was severely beaten and returned minus a few teeth, remains a family mystery.

Getting expelled from a country she had learned to love was a new experience for my mom Nancy, who, living in remote Medan, was removed from the complexities of post-independence Indonesian politics. The anti-Dutch campaign was launched days after the United Nations General Assembly on November 29, 1957, failed to pass an Indonesian resolution to spur the Netherlands into a new round of talks over Irian Barat (West Irian), also known as Dutch New Guinea, and nowadays as West Papua, the western half of the huge island of New Guinea. The resolution failed to win the assembly's required two-thirds support, and so was dropped. The next day, President Sukarno narrowly escaped a grenade assassination attempt while leaving a school function in Jakarta. The explosions claimed nine dead, including children. The attack was eventually blamed on Muslim extremists, although authorities suspected the assassins were secretly backed by the Dutch.[1]

In retaliation for the UN rejection, the Indonesian government immediately banned Dutch citizens from entering the country. Dutch-language newspapers and magazines were shut down. Labor strikes broke out simultaneously at thousands of Dutch-owned companies and estates nationwide. Some companies were seized by their employees, who proceeded to loot them. Stores and restaurants in Jakarta and Surabaya, the two main cities in Java, refused to serve Dutch clients, and authorities confiscated goods from

European and Indonesian neighbors who attempted to help the Dutch by secretly sharing their own supplies. Dutch people went hungry. Later, the government cut off electricity and water supplies to Dutch homes. Dutch people went without a shower.

On December 5, 1957, the government announced plans to nationalize all Dutch-owned companies and expel an estimated 46,000 Dutch nationals residing throughout the vast resource-rich archipelago, known as the Dutch East Indies since 1800. The Dutch had ruled Indonesia for 340 years, first under the ruthlessly mercantile East Indies Company (VOC) (1602-1800), followed by colonial rule (1800 to 1942), after the VOC went bankrupt. Although Dutch supremacy in Indonesia had practically ended with the invasion of Java by the Japanese army in March 1942 and the seven-day battle ending in a humiliating defeat for the Dutch armed forces, colonial rule only officially ended on December 27, 1949 when Amsterdam begrudgingly recognized Indonesian independence.

The new Indonesian government gave the Dutch and Eurasians—the mixed blood offspring of European and Indonesian ancestry—two years to decide whether they wanted to assume Indonesian citizenship or remain Dutch and leave the country. Thousands of Dutch and Eurasians lingered on beyond the 1951 deadline, many of them feeling more at home in the Indonesian archipelago—called the "Emerald Girdle" by the Dutch—than elsewhere. Others stayed for the job opportunities, which were scarce in post-World War II Holland. "We've been here for 340 years. We'll stay for 340 more," was a common refrain among the Dutch community. They were wrong about that.

The Netherlands had refused to include West New Guinea under the 1949 independence agreement, arguing that the territory was historically, culturally and ethnically distinct from Indonesia and deserved its own independence, eventually. This exclusion of West New Guinea would prove a thorn in the side of the already prickly post-independence Dutch-Indonesian relations and an easy target for Sukarno's anti-colonial, anti-Dutch diatribes. Sukarno, Indonesia's charismatic president from 1945 to 1967, argued that West New Guinea, and most of South-east Asia for that matter, had been conquered by the Surabaya-based Majapahit empire (1293-1500) and must be returned to independent Indonesia. Sukarno, who was born in Surabaya, used radio broadcasts to stir up the emotions of the Indonesian masses. My mother recorded one such broadcast.

> "*Saudara, Saudari* (brothers/sisters)," Sukarno began in a soft voice. "Listen to me," pause. "What do I see?" louder. "I see a distant shoreline," louder still. "With some *kelapa* (coconut) trees," pause. "And a small hut where children are playing," pause. "And I want to go to that shore with those *kelapa* trees and those small children playing," louder. "But I cannot," pause. "For where is that shore and those *kelapa* trees and those children?" louder. "That shore and *kelapa* trees and children are in," pause, "IRIAN BARAT," crescendo."
>
> *Diary entry, December 1, 1957.*

Indonesians would also suffer from the crackdown on Dutch enterprises which then still accounted for the lion's share of the economy. In 1938, Dutch private investments in the archipelago had amounted to an estimated

2.8 billion guilders and produced about 7.4 percent of Holland's national income.[2] Indonesia was a major producer of commodities and accounted for 8.6 percent of world trade in 1928,[3] compared with 1 percent in 2013. For the USA, Indonesia accounted for 50 percent of its rubber imports, 10 percent of tin, 90 percent of quinine, 80 percent of palm oil and 25 percent of tea.[4] In the USA, Java was synonymous with coffee, and tobacco from Deli, North Sumatra, was known as "the world's best wrapper". The Dutch were world traders and Indonesia was their main source of raw materials.

In their agreement to grant Indonesia independence in 1949, signed by Indonesian Prime Minister Mohammed Hatta, the Dutch had not only clung to West New Guinea but also to their significant economic interests in their former colony, demanding assurances of protection for their investments and special status as most-favored-nation in trade. For its part, the Indonesian government demanded that Dutch firms employ and train more local staff for management posts. While Hatta, a devout Muslim and a champion of the Indonesian territories outside of Java, was a proponent of gradual disengagement from Dutch economic interests, Sukarno had other ideas.

In 1950, an estimated 226,000 Europeans were still living and working in the newly independent Indonesia,[5] forming a privileged class in a swiftly deteriorating environment for the Indonesian masses, who had already suffered severe deprivations under the Japanese occupation in World War II. Although Indonesians had been spared the Japanese concentration camps, unlike the Dutch and other Europeans barring the Germans, the occupation had led to widespread food shortages, as rice and other necessities were funneled into the Japanese war machine. An estimated 4 million Indonesians were pressed into service for the Japanese war effort, some of them sent to work on the notorious Death Railway in Thailand and Burma (Myanmar). An estimated 70,000 of these so-called *remushas* died. Famine stalked the land in 1944-1945.

During the war, there were shortages of everything including clothing. People went about clad in gunnysacks and banana leaves.[6] In a bid to keep the population on their side, the Japanese allowed Sukarno and Hatta to proclaim Indonesia independent on August 17, 1945, two days after the Japanese announced they would surrender. It would take four years, British intervention, a few bloody battles and dwindling international support for the Dutch before they would ratify that independence.

Later, the Dutch would try to relocate the hundreds of thousands of Indos—as the Eurasians were known— to West New Guinea, the initial, misguided step in their doomed New Guinea diplomacy. Few Indos wanted to live in the backwater Dutch New Guinea, hardly a land of gold. (Guinea was the Portuguese name of sub-Saharan Africa, where a vast gold mine was fabled to be but which was never found). Thousands would migrate to Australia, Holland and the USA instead.

While fighting broke out between the nascent Indonesian army and the returning Dutch, there were widespread shortages of food and other necessities and meagre revenues from exports as the economy limped back to semi-normalcy. The post-1949 independence period was a process of Indonesia reclaiming its economic sovereignty from the Dutch after three and a half centuries of colonialism, culminating in the blanket nationalization of all Dutch properties and businesses in 1957, including my family's tobacco and rubber plantations in North Sumatra.

By July 1951, Dutch ownership of the vast plantation sector of tobacco, rubber, palm oil, coffee and tea had decreased to 51.5 percent from 63 percent in 1929.[7] By 1958, it would be zero. But profits were good for the Sumatran plantation belt in the post-independence period, aided by the Korean War (1950 to 1953), which boosted commodity prices, especially that of rubber, which had become the dominant crop, surpassing tobacco in acreage.

During the period 1950 to 1957, the Janssen-Cremer fortunes were on an upswing. My mother would arrive in North Sumatra in May 1953, just in time to experience four years of renewed Dutch optimism about their future in Indonesia. My father entertained hopes of one day taking over the tobacco operations of the Senembah Maatschappij (Senembah Company), started by his great uncle, Christian Janssen. Those dreams would be dashed by Sukarno, who was bent on seeing the last of the Dutch.

In March 1957, Sukarno had decided that parliamentary democracy was unworkable in Indonesia and introduced his concept of "guided democracy," with himself very much at the helm.[8] By December, Sukarno was ready to demonstrate his new powers by booting the Dutch out of Indonesia once and for all. Although no doubt a worthy and noble cause for any Indonesian nationalist, Dutch politicians questioned his motives. Dutch Ambassador to Washington D.C. J.H. van Roijen in a televised interview on December 8, 1957, called Sukarno's anti-Dutch campaign over the West New Guinea issue a diversionary tactic to unite the Indonesian people behind him by making the Dutch a "scapegoat"[9] for his failure to revive the economy and improve people's lives. "New Guinea is neither geo-graphically nor ethnically any more a part of Indonesia than Ceylon [Sri Lanka] is of India," the ambassador said. "I am convinced that Sukarno is a great opportunist and a consummate demagogue."

In response to the Dutch ambassador's accusation, the Indonesian embassy in Washington D.C. issued a statement the following day, saying: "The patience of the Indonesian people has been put to a test for hundreds of years during the Dutch rule since the beginning of the 17th century. This patience is now exhausted".[10] In Jakarta, Sukarno stood his ground. He warned of looming shortages of food, clothing and other vital goods, but concluded, "We are not making any compromises with colonial countries".[11] He then took a two-week holiday, sparking wishful rumors in Holland that he had been overthrown by the military. They proved premature, by eight years. That would only happen in 1965, although Sukarno would remain titular president until 1967.

Ultimately, the brunt of the anti-Dutch campaign would be borne by the long-suffering Indonesian people. For instance, the nationalization of the Koninklijke Paket-vaart Maatschappij (KPM), the shipping line established by Dutch investors in 1888, which by 1957 controlled more than 70 percent of Indonesia's seafaring traffic, would prove particularly disruptive. In a bid to prevent the vessels from leaving Indonesian waters, the government placed plain-clothes military officers on board. The KPM quickly shifted its headquarters from Jakarta to Singapore.

Although most of the KPM ships had only a handful of Dutch nationals working on them, they still commanded the top jobs of captain, first mate and head mechanic. When these key officials staged their own strike to protest the nationalization, service suffered. In a show of solidarity, other Dutch liners plying the Holland-Indonesia route stopped entering Indonesian waters, leading to shortages of foodstuffs, equipment, spare parts, petrol and luxury items while undermining Indonesia's vital exports. The disruption of the KPM intra-island services had a more direct impact on food supplies, such as rice—the staple of the national diet. Inflation soared.

> "Despite its potential richness, in Indonesia it is still nec-
> essary to import all the staples of life, not to mention the
> simplest luxuries or manufactured items. The nationalization
> of the KPM and the repercussions therefrom cut the ties
> among the islands as well as the principal ties with the out-
> side world. The onus of hunger jumped, real and threatening.
> The rush to hoard was on and prices shot through the ceiling.
> In Jakarta, by mid-December, a kilogram of rice sold for
> 13.50 rupiahs, the average monthly wage for plantation
> workers. A family of four consumed about 20 kilograms
> of the grain. North Sumatra was in a slightly better shape,
> with four months' supply in storage and the local paddy
> fields just ripening. Of course, that did not stop profiteering.
> Chinese shopkeepers withheld their stock to force prices
> up or sold quick and fast for fear of military confiscation."
> *Diary entry, December 11, 1957.*

By 1957, there was a large Chinese population in Medan and the surrounding districts, many of them descendants of "coolie" laborers on the plantations who were initially recruited, or conscripted, from Asia's port cities—Penang, Hong Kong, Singapore, Swatow and Shanghai. Their "recruitment" was necessary because Sumatra lacked a significant domestic labor force, and the indigenous Malays and Bataks were not keen on strenuous work, understandably. From 1870 to 1933, about 300,000 Chinese had migrated to the Deli region.[12] The Chinese were the plantations' original indentured labor force, labeled "coolies," a word that is believed to have derived from *kulhi*, the name of a tribe native to Gujarat, India, who worked as day laborers. Although viewed as industrious, the Chinese "coolies" were also seen as troublemakers, and were eventually replaced by Javanese, who had been forced to seek employment outside their over-populated island.

Herbert Janssen, my father, and Nancy Janssen, my mother, who spent the first four years of their marriage in North Sumatra.

In the 1930s, the overseas Chinese had largely graduated out of the plantation belt, where labor conditions, especially in the early years, were likened to modern-day slavery. They moved into the towns and took up more lucrative vocations such as running shops and restaurants in the city. Medan today still has a vibrant Chinese restaurant scene, centered in the Jalan Kesawan neighborhood which was the site of the original Chinatown.

A handful of Chinese would become millionaires, such as Tjong A Fie, who dominated Medan's real estate market and eventually invested his vast profits in the plantations that fueled the Sumatran economy. The Chinese in Medan would also feel the whip of Indonesian nationalism, but only after the fall of Sukarno in 1965 and the subsequent anti-communist campaign that would claim somewhere between 500,000 and 1 million lives, many of them ethnic Chinese. But in December 1957, the Chinese community was generally spared in the crackdown on the Dutch, although Chinese-language schools were forced to close in a clampdown on all foreign-language schools.

"Right before the nationalization of the KPM, a significant step was taken in regard to schools. From one day to the next, the order was issued that all Indonesian children in foreign schools must transfer to government schools. This must be done within three weeks' time. And teachers in foreign schools were required to pay a stiff new tax. Indonesians were only permitted to study in their own language under the new government study plan. This dictate included missionary schools which, although under a foreign language were filled mainly with Indonesians. The dictate also included Chinese schools, by far the largest number of non-Indonesian-language schools. The amalgamation of the Chinese-Indonesians is an old-standing problem, mutually strengthened by the resistance of both groups to give up their idea of separateness... We asked our better Indonesian friends what had happened to their freedom, but not one of them raised a complaint worth mentioning."

Diary entry, December 11, 1957.

The Indonesian government, which had rushed to nationalize all Dutch firms without sufficient planning, was peeved by Dutch efforts to save their assets. At The Hague, the Indonesian government on December 12, 1957, issued a statement via its embassy, expressing its regret that the KPM had moved its headquarters to Singapore and ordered its ships not to serve the archipelago—then an estimated at 13,700 islands, but now put at 17,000. "The result of KPM's rash step is stagnation in goods and passenger traffic," said the statement.[13] "The Indonesian government never intended to confiscate KPM ships. It has never been the intention of the Indonesian government to expel 46,000 Dutch from the country. The Dutch government is merely being requested to repatriate all unemployed Dutch nationals." Of course, since the government had decided to nationalize all Dutch enterprises and revoke all work permits, none of the remaining 46,000 Dutch people were officially employed.

For the Dutch employees of the Medan-based Senembah Company, established in 1889 by Christian Wilhelm Janssen, a great uncle of mine, it was the end of an era of a family fortune based on cheap labor, and tobacco, rubber and palm oil grown in the Deli district's rich, alluvial soil. The Senembah Company was officially signed over to a military-led Indonesian management on December 14, 1957, terminating the employment and shattering the ambitions of my father Herbert Janssen, whose father, Peter William Janssen II, was the company's managing director.

By mid-December, the Janssens wanted to get out. All the Janssen family members working in Sumatra, and many of the Dutch employees, had spent years in the Japanese concentration camps in Indonesia during World War II, and had no desire to find out if Sukarno had some concentration camp plans of his own in mind for the Dutch who failed to obey his marching orders. In Jakarta, relief centers were set up to handle the thousands of Dutch who streamed into the capital from the Javanese countryside and outlying islands who couldn't get airplane tickets out of the county because KLM had been ejected and Garuda refused to take Dutch passengers. Peter W. Janssen II and his second wife Lutske Nicolai, visited Jakarta in early December to assess the situation and look into the possibility of keeping their hold on the Senembah Company. They returned to Medan with bad news.

> "Jakarta was like a tomb. Westerners stayed in their houses, streets were deserted, the atmosphere hysterical. And still Sumatra blithely felt itself to be different."
> *Diary entry, December 13, 1957.*

In North Sumatra, confusion prevailed as the Jakarta-based policies crept up the huge island to Medan. Various political movements sought to take advantage of the chaos with secret and hopeless schemes of seceding from Java, but these rumblings were soon quieted when the Indonesian military moved in and took charge of the local government and the Dutch-owned plantations.

Medan, nowadays Indonesia's fifth most populous city, was put on the global map by the Deli Company, which chose the slightly inland village of Medan Puteri as the location for its headquarters. The first office was in a classic Indonesian *pangjung*—house on stilts—erected in 1869. Nienhuys chose Medan Puteri because it sat at the confluence of the Deli and Babura rivers, allowing small boats to travel to the nearby harbor on the Sumatran east coast to collect cargo and unload bales of tobacco.[14]

Medan would be transformed into a cosmopolitan entrepot and the commercial hub of one of the most successful economic adventures to spring from the colonial era. "Over the past century Sumatra has become the site of one of the most intensive and successful pursuits of foreign agricultural enterprise in the Third World," wrote Ann Laura Stoler.[15] "It was and remains the densest concentration of multinational agribusiness in Southeast Asia."[16]

Medan became the official capital of North Sumatra in 1891, when the then Sultan of Deli, Makmum Al Rasjif, moved his residence from Laboehan to the Maimoon Palace, now a major tourist attraction in Medan. The city's wealth was rooted in the plantation belt that surrounded it—vast expanses of 300,000 hectares of tobacco, rubber and palm oil estates owned by Dutch, European and American companies and maintained by "coolie" laborers. The plantations were described as "a state within a state," empowered by the 1880 Coolie Ordinance, the brainchild of my great-great grandfather Jacob Theodore Cremer, to mete out harsh penalties on the indentured laborers recruited chiefly from China and Java for offenses such as running away, shirking, talking back to the bosses, organizing labor unions and buying stuff from the market instead of company stores.

The mistreatment of the laborers, legalized by the Coolie Ordinance, would become notorious with the publication of *The Millions from Deli* pamphlet by the Medan-based Dutch lawyer Johannes van den Brand. The pamphlet would tarnish the names of two of my ancestors, Jacob Theodore Cremer and Peter Janssen I, in Holland, leading to the end of the active political career of the former and the transformation into a philanthropist of the latter.

The true pioneer of the tobacco industry in Deli, North Sumatra, was Nienhuys, a Dutch tobacco trader whose first business adventure in Surabaya was floundering. Induced by an Arab trader, Nienhuys travelled in 1863 to Deli, where he was granted a 20-year concession by the sultan of Deli[17] to grow a small crop of tobacco and purchase the plant from the natives. In March 1864, he took 50 bales of his Deli tobacco to Rotterdam, in the Netherlands, where merchants snapped them up, impressed with the quality of the leaf. But Nienhuys failed to persuade Dutch merchants to invest in an expansion of his tobacco plantation in Deli. The tobacco traders were eager to buy more but shied away from the risks of investment in an exotic land.

Nienhuys had better luck in Amsterdam, where "over a beer" he met G.C. Clemens, a close friend of Peter Wilhelm Janssen I, my great-great grandfather, a German-born grain merchant who would take Dutch nationality in 1865. In his mid-40s and already wealthy, Janssen was interested in Nienhuys' tobacco venture, but cautious. He sent Clemens back to Sumatra with Nienhuys to conduct due diligence. Clemens reported back on the project enthusiastically, then died of dysentery, a common complaint in Medan.

Janssen provided Nienhuys with 30,000 guilders to plant tobacco, and in 1867 earned a net profit of 37,000 guilders when they sold their first crop in Amsterdam. In December 1869, Nienhuys and Janssen listed the Deli Maatschappij (Deli Company) on the Amsterdam bourse. It was the first Dutch East Indies-based enterprise to be listed on the Dutch stock exchange. Janssen, who would later be dubbed the "King of Deli," because of the vast fortune he made there, never once visited Sumatra during his lifetime, perhaps mindful of his friend Clemens' fate.

Nienhuys would be forced to flee North Sumatra in early 1871 after he was indicted for beating seven Chinese coolies to death.[18] He returned to Holland where he became a commissioner of the Deli Company and a very wealthy man. To replace Nienhuys in Medan, the company hired the young Jacob Theodore Cremer, another great-great grandfather of mine, who was then an employee of the Dutch Trading Company's office in Batavia (the Japanese would change the name to Jakarta during the WWII occupation). He became the managing director of the Deli Company at the age of 24 and would make the firm financially successful. On average, a dividend of 73 percent of profits was paid annually from 1871 to 1883, according to company records. When Cremer returned to Holland in 1883, he got involved in politics, eventually rising to become minister of the colonies from 1897 to 1901.

The Deli Company became a well-known name in Amsterdam, and the pioneering spirit and successful business partnership of Nienhuys, Janssen and Cremer was romanticized in the popular novel, *The Earth of Deli (De aarde von Deli)*, by William Brandt (1948). He wrote of the three men, "Nienhuys was the pioneer, Janssen the man of faith and Cremer the builder."

While the Deli Company was the largest tobacco operation in North Sumatra, the Senembah Company became the second largest. Senembah was started by Janssen's eldest son, Christian Wilhelm Janssen (1860 to 1927) in collaboration with executives of the Deli Company, including Cremer and Nienhuys. Unlike his father, Christian was fond of traveling and first visited Sumatra in 1883. After finishing his Ph.D. at Strasbourg University, where his thesis was *The Dutch Colonial Economy in the Bataklands of Sumatra*, he returned to Sumatra to mind the family business interests.

Here Christian Janssen and board members of the Deli Company bought up a tobacco plantation owned by a German and Swiss partnership. With the backing of the Deli Company, the Senembah Company was listed on the Amsterdam bourse, with the major shareholders including the two previous owners, Janssen and Nienhuys. To the directors' surprise, the Senembah Company became a financial success. "The Senembah Maatschappij intended to be a simple continuation of a quite large existing company without having great expectations," said a company publication of its startup. Between the years 1889 and 1912, the Deli and Senembah companies together accounted for the lion's share of North Sumatra's tobacco production, with Senembah actually surpassing Deli Company's output one year, in 1895.

After being shut down during World War II, and having much of their tobacco plantation lands used for agriculture to feed the local population, the Deli and Senembah companies had enjoyed a rebirth in the 1950s, fueled by growing demand for rubber because of the Korean War, and healthy exports of tobacco and palm oil as well. The renewed fortunes gave rise to hopes that the boom days were back, especially for my father, Herbert, who had dropped out of college in the US to join the family-run Senembah business. Nepotism was the norm in those days. According to Senembah Company records, seen by my step-uncle Wouter Nicolai when he was working as a World Bank consultant in the 1980s, Herbert was being groomed to take over the tobacco side of the plantation business, while Wouter, his step-brother, was in line to manage the company's palm oil and rubber plantation. Neither job would materialize.

By the second week of December 1957, the reality of the Dutch expulsion began to sink in in Medan, where Dutch companies were closed for days due to labor strikes. While Dutch families were openly persecuted in Java, where they were denied food and utilities, the worst they seemed to suffer in North Sumatra was a few death threats and a lack of maids, who had been instructed to stay away from their Dutch employers. A proficient cook herself, with or without servants, my mother prepared a big dinner for my father's 27th birthday on December 4, with 16 friends invited.

"Herb was a real birthday child, hungry for the good dinner, afraid that he would not get enough, because although everyone had eaten, they still ate more out of politeness. He was at the tail end of the line and sat in the corner eating his chicken leg. It was a good and quiet party, with people rather subdued by the news but not distressed. It was still the time when everyone took satisfaction in the gathering mess and were not shrouded in to silence by the seriousness of the times,"

Diary entry, December 4, 1957.

The Dutch community in Medan held a St. Nicolas Eve party on December 5, with the usual suspects in attendance—a white bearded Santa Claus and his faithful assistant—*Zwarte Piet* (Black Pete). It was a big event for the children, including Josie Janssen, my sister, born on April 29, 1954. On previous occasions Josie had found Santa Claus and *Zwarte Piet* terrifying, but this Christmas she was showing her three and a half years.

> "Josie looked adorable and enjoyed herself. Riding home alone with me, she reassured herself—'*Josie niet takut*, (Josie was not afraid).' '*Josie takut buat Santa Klaus* (Josie was afraid of Santa Claus)?' Sisu, (her Indonesian nanny), asked her the following day. '*Tidah. Klaus tidah bikin apa apa*, (No. Claus didn't do anything).'"
>
> *Diary entry, December 6, 1957.*

My sister, in her first years spoke mostly Dutch and Indonesian, a result of spending a lot of time with the servants. The servants also gave her a healthy fear of ghosts and other spooky figures, such as Santa Claus and *Zwarte Piet*. A year after leaving Sumatra, Josie would have forgotten her Indonesian, but it would take half a lifetime to lose her fear of ghosts and the dark.

On December 7, the Indonesian military took control of the Senembah Company, setting up a committee of military men and Indonesian managers to handle the takeover. Koos Schoon, the not-so-popular General Manager of Senembah, and a distant relative of my grandfather's, was called in that day for the first meeting with the military committee, two officers and one Indonesian manager that were taking over the company 'to protect the property.'

My mother and father and sister—Josie Janssen, in North Sumatra.

"And so began the catapult of events to a dramatic conclusion. We were still hopeful that it was a good sign. The military were behaving well and we told each other that some Indonesians realized the mistake and were putting a stop to it. Sumatra would remain reasonable. But we were wrong. The ball was now gathering speed."

Diary entry, December 16, 1957.

Anticipating the worst, Schoon in early December managed to lose the records of a recent shipment of 1,700 bales of tobacco to Bremen, Germany, from the company's account books. Janssen had approved the transaction, although it was illegal and would lead to a lawsuit later. The sleight-of-hand would put pressure on Schoon and Janssen to get out of Medan fast, before the transaction was discovered. Besides the unaccounted for 1,700 bales of tobacco, Janssen and his second wife Lutske Nicolai were worried about being held hostage for ransom.

> "Lutske told me Papa had been warned in the AVROS (Sumatran Planters Association) to leave quickly. Behind his glasses I had seen tears in Papa's eyes. The war had left him with bitter memories and I knew it was hard for him to risk it again."
>
> *Diary entry, December 16, 1957.*

My grandfather had been held in solitary confinement and tortured by the Japanese during the first months of the occupation of Sumatra in 1942. Although he never talked about the experience, it was assumed they were torturing him in the hopes of his divulging where he hid his wealth, not for military secrets.

Peter W. Janssen II, whom I always called Opa, was a tall and strikingly good-looking man. He had a fine aquiline nose, and kept his long hair combed straight back from the forehead. Before marrying Jetske Cremer, his first wife, he had a reputation for being one of the handsomest, wealthiest men in Holland. But he was not a great businessman. He drifted into the family tobacco business in the footsteps of his father, August Janssen, who had taken over the directorship of the Senembah Company, from his elder brother Christian Janssen, one of the founders.

Opa had a romantic streak. He went to see the Hollywood film Gigi, about a French aristocrat who falls in love with a young, vivacious courtesan-in-training, at least 16 times. Before the war he had fallen in love with Lutske Nicolai, the voluptuous, extroverted wife of Constans

*Peter William Janssen II, my grandfather, and descendant of
Peter Wilhelm Janssen I, who dared to invest in the first tobacco
plantation in Deli, North Sumatra.*

Nicolai, a Dutch lawyer. The two became an "item" at the Medan Societeit Club. After the war and the years in the concentration camps, Janssen tried to patch up his marriage with Jetske but it didn't work. By 1951, they had divorced, causing a scandal in Medan which didn't help his already strained business relations with the Cremers. He married Lutske in 1953, months before the marriage of my parents. Opa was fond of my mother, whom he hoped would have a good influence on his sometimes unruly son.

The 1957 expulsion brought the Dutch community together. Typical of the times was my mother's coffee break with "Papa" on December 12 at the Tip Top Restaurant, the nerve center of the nervous Dutch and European community in Medan, and still a popular gathering place in Medan today. Father-in-law and daughter-in-law were joined by Mr. Pol, the tennis instructor. Nancy teased Pol about all the money he would soon be making off his wealthy Indonesian students, but the tennis coach was not so sure.

> "Despite his *warna negara* (citizenship), Indonesian wife and five children, he said he would still be a white man when the going got tough. He was in a bad spot and knew it."
> *Diary entry, December 13, 1957.*

Papa and Lutske were booked on a flight to Singapore on December 14, a Saturday, to be accompanied by their two grandchildren, my sister and me. Nancy had originally objected to being parted from her children, but had finally given in, in light of the growing political uncertainties and mad scramble by the Dutch community to get their papers in order to leave the country. Nancy and Herbert were to

be among the last among the Senembah employees to leave
Sumatra, on January 4, 1958.

> "Herb had become annoyed with all the hysteria. He would
> stay until the end, the bitter end."
>> *Diary entry, December 16, 1957.*

A last-minute surprise was the decision by Schoon, the
general manager of the Senembah Company, to join Papa
and Lutske on the December 14 flight out. Schoon, having
conveniently lost 1,700 bales of tobacco in the company's
accounts book, was keen to leave quickly and had not adver-
tised his departure plans to the Indonesians. On the morning
of the 14th he was summoned to the Senembah Company
headquarters in Medan to sign over ownership of the firm to
the Indonesian government, represented by a military-run
management committee. That day would be the last time
the personnel were paid under full Senembah supervision.

Schoon signed the papers bequeathing the 68-year-old
Senembah Company to Indonesia, but "under protest," to
keep the legality of the transaction in question. The Indonesian side would have some questions of their own in the
near future.

> "When they opened the cash box it was only to find a
> debt of 36,000,000 rupiahs to the Bank of Indonesia and
> no legal receipt for the 1,700 bales of tobacco which had
> already been sent."
>> *Diary entry, December 16, 1957.*

But by the time this happened, Schoon and his wife Ietje,
would be on the airplane to Singapore. Also aboard the

flight on December 14 were Peter W. Janssen II, Lutske, Josie Janssen (my sister) and Peter W. Janssen III (me). Herbert and Nancy watched their departure at Medan Airport.

"Ietje (Schoon's wife) had made a ponytail for Josie and when they finally left she marched out to the plane with the red ribbon bouncing purposefully. PW went with Lutske. Through the plane window you could see Lutske sit down and he leaned his tired round face against her breast. They left and the nervous tension of the last few days began to subside. We went home."

Diary entry, December 16, 1957.

CHAPTER 3

LEAVING BEHIND THE FAMILY LEGACY IN DELI

My parents left Medan on January 4, 1958, for Singapore, where they were forced to spend two weeks, along with thousands of other Dutch evacuees, awaiting a flight to Amsterdam for a reunion with their family. Their hurried departure marked the closure of the most hopeful phase of their marriage, an odd pairing of a descendent of two of the wealthiest Dutch colonialist clans in Sumatra and an idealistic, young, liberal American woman born on a farm in New Jersey and educated at Sarah Lawrence College.

The Dutch left behind a bad taste that would linger in Indonesia for generations. "Don't wear shorts—ever. The Dutch wore shorts," the veteran Australian journalist Wally O'Sullivan advised newcomer Guy Hamilton in the opening chapter of *The Year of Living Dangerously*, by Christopher J. Koch, a novel set in Jakarta in 1965. Dutch journalists were banned at the time. Sukarno would sever all diplomatic ties with the Netherlands on August 17, 1960, in his escalated campaign to claim West New Guinea for Indonesia.

Under increasing pressure from the international commu-
nity, including its main allies the USA and Britain, the
Netherlands finally signed an accord with Indonesia on
July 28, 1963, to hand over the sovereignty of West New
Guinea, ending once and for all their colonial presence in
the vast archipelago.

Ironically, the victory would contribute to Sukarno's
eventual downfall on September 30, 1965, in a military
coup. "After the nationalization of the Dutch business sector
and the vast armaments purchasing program the national
economy continued to deteriorate, pushing the nation into
bankruptcy and causing widespread poverty, starvation, mal-
nutrition and disease," C.L.M. Penders wrote in his book
The West New Guinea Debacle.[19] "The West Irian victory
turned out to be one of the major causes of Sukarno's fall,
and in contrast to the expectations of the Indonesian left,
the destruction of Dutch economic power in Indonesia had
not plunged the Dutch economy into the expected disar-
ray."[20] The West Papuans were arguably the biggest losers in
the debacle. Their doomed struggle for independence con-
tinues today. Indonesia's diplomatic ties were restored with
the Netherlands in 1968 by its new leader, General Suharto,
whose autocratic, pro-capitalist, corruption-plagued rule
would last until 1998.

The evicted Dutch families from Indonesia would return
to an unsympathetic homeland. In the late 1950s, the Netherlands was looking to Europe as its new engine of growth,
and the public was largely ashamed of its colonial past in
the Dutch East Indies and contemptuous of the entrepreneurs who had made their millions, or *Indisch Fortuin*
(Indies Fortunes) off Indonesian labor and the country's
abundant resources.

And the Cremers and Janssens were classic examples of *Indisch Fortuin*, earning the families almost legendary status, and some notoriety, in the Netherlands. Their legacies remain a mixed bag of praise as pioneering capitalists, carving a tobacco empire out of the Sumatran jungle, and condemnation as ruthless exploiters of "coolie" labor. As recently as July 2014, the magazine *Our Amsterdam* published a lengthy article on my great-great grandfather, Peter Wilhelm Janssen (1821-1903) under the headline *The Philanthrope, Parvenu and Thousands of Poor Devils*. The first revelation in the article, usually hushed up by my Dutch relatives in their own accounts of the family history, was that Peter Wilhelm Janssen (Wilhelm with an 'h') was not Dutch by birth. He was born in 1821 on the small island of Wangerooge in the East Frisian Islands in northern Germany. He received a business education in Bremen, Germany, and then as a young man of twenty-two migrated to Amsterdam in 1843, where he would live for the rest of his life and amass at least two fortunes, one founded on a lucky mistake and the other on a deliberate and successful gamble.

In Amsterdam, Janssen first toyed with the idea of going to the Dutch East Indies to seek his fortune, but instead he became an apprentice at the Lavino tobacco company in Amsterdam. Seven years later, he started his own trading company with two other German migrants, specializing in selling grain to the "East Sea counties," i.e. the islands off northern Germany. His first fortune was a result of a lucky mistake. "He ordered two shipments of grain, but because of a misunderstanding twenty fully loaded ships were waiting for him at the port of Amsterdam," wrote *Our Amsterdam* magazine. "Fortunately, the price of grain rose steeply,

resulting in a great profit for him." In 1853, he married
Folmina Margaretha Peters, daughter of another German
migrant who owned a factory that processed kapok—a
fibrous substance similar to cotton that grows around the
seeds of the ceiba tree and is used as stuffing for cush-
ions. Janssen took over the factory after his father-in-law's
death and, amazingly, it survived, under various owners,
until 1992.

By the time he was 46 years old, Janssen was already a
wealthy grain merchant, boasting a house in the respectable Keizersgracht neighborhood of Amsterdam. He and
his two sons, Christian and August, took Dutch nationality in 1865, presumably to avoid his sons' conscription
into the Prussian army. In 1867, Janssen was to embark on

My great-great grandfather Peter Wilhelm Janssen and his wife
Folmina Peters Janssen.

a new business venture that would transform him from a respectable grain merchant into the reputed "King of Deli" and one of Amsterdam's wealthiest denizens, and eventually, one of its most generous philanthropists, albeit limiting his largesse to Holland and his native Friesland.

The Janssen-Cremer legacy in Sumatra is closely linked to that of another legendary Dutchman, Jacob Nienhuys (1836-1927). He is credited with the "discovery" of North Sumatra's suitability for growing tobacco, according to the corporate creed as described by Dutch author Willem Brandt (pseudonym of W.S.B. Klooster, a former civil servant in North Sumatra) in his historical novel *The Earth of Deli* published in 1948. The novel paints a rather rosy picture of the Deli Company and its founders as adventurers, pioneers and hard-working capitalists.

According to *The Earth of Deli* legend, Nienhuys was an entrepreneur-adventurer who traveled to Sumatra where he discovered the rich volcanic soil is perfect for tobacco cultivation and persuaded the local Sultan to grant him a 20-year lease to grow it in the Deli district. He grew a sample crop in 1864 and sold it in Rotterdam, where the tobacco merchants snapped it up, but were reluctant to lend Nienhuys money to invest in a tobacco plantation.

Nienhuys bumped into Peter Wilhelm Janssen who lent him 30,000 guilders (the equivalent of several hundred thousand dollars nowadays). With the money, Nienhuys returned to North Sumatra, and cultivated and harvested a tobacco crop. They sold it in Amsterdam for 67,000 guilders, earning a 37,000-guilder net profit, and the Deli Company was born on November 1, 1869. The Deli Company went on to become one of Holland's most profitable colonial investments and the Janssen fortune was made.

Not everyone agrees with this corporate version of the Deli Company genesis. Indonesian historians have a slightly different take on the story. For starters, Nienhuys did not chance upon the tobacco potential of North Sumatra by Dutch business acumen or happenstance but was lured to the area by Deli Sultan Mahmoed Parkasa Alam Shah, who ruled from 1861 to 1873.

According to the Indonesian historian Tengku Luckman Sinar, the European "discovery" of tobacco in Sumatra was really attributable to Syed Abdullah Bilsagih, a Surabaya merchant of Arab origin. Bilsagih had gone bankrupt in Surabaya and was shipwrecked off the coast of North Sumatra en route to Calcutta.[21] He adapted well to his new home, and soon married the sister of the sultan, whom he persuaded to use tobacco to attract Dutch investors to Deli. The sultan was keen to draw the Dutch to the Deli region to strengthen his hand against local rivals in Aceh and Riau, neighboring sultanates.

Tobacco, although indigenous to the Americas, had been grown in the Deli region by Malay farmers and Batak tribesmen for decades. As early as 1823, John Anderson, a Penang-based employee of the British East India Company, already recounted seeing fields of tobacco in his *Mission to the East Coast of Sumatra* report. "Large parties of Malays were clearing away the jungle, as we passed, for the purpose of planting tobacco, of which we observed several small plantations in a thriving state," Anderson wrote.[22]

Bilsagih was dispatched to Jakarta to seek Dutch investors, but he failed to muster interest there. He had more luck in Surabaya, where he caught the attention of Nienhuys, whose Surabaya tobacco venture there was floundering. Nienhuys travelled in 1863 to Deli, where he was granted a 20-year concession by the sultan to grow a small crop of tobacco and purchase the plant from the natives.[23] In 1864, he took his tobacco samples to Holland where he eventually hooked up with Janssen, after meeting G.C. Clemens, a close friend of Janssen's, at an Amsterdam beerhouse. Janssen dispatched Clemens to Sumatra with Nienhuys to conduct some due diligence on the tobacco scheme. Clemens promptly died of dysentery after recommending Janssen invest the legendary 30,000 guilders. Throughout his life Janssen never visited Sumatra, perhaps heeding the unfortunate lesson of Clemens.

Nienhuys was also the first to pioneer to use "coolie" labor in the tobacco fields. Although the crop was already being grown by Malay and Batak farmers, Nienhuys found that maintaining the quality standard of the locally purchased tobacco was difficult, so he decided he needed to invest in larger plantations under his own control. But the local Malay and Batak had little interest in working on them. Because of the labor shortage, Nienhuys started importing Chinese workers from nearby Penang. These Chinese "coolies" also took umbrage with the backbreaking work, apparently. In 1871, Nienhuys was forced to flee Sumatra after being indicted for beating seven Chinese laborers to death.

"Nienhuys was forced to leave not for reasons of health, which was the story told to outsiders, but in order to escape prosecutors because of a crime he had committed, which was the flogging of some coolies to death," the Dutch sociologist and historian Jan Breman, wrote in his seminal book, *Taming the Coolie Beast*.[24] The Deli Company asked for a fresh investigation into the case in 1875, hoping to clear Nienhuys' name, but the Dutch official responsible for the

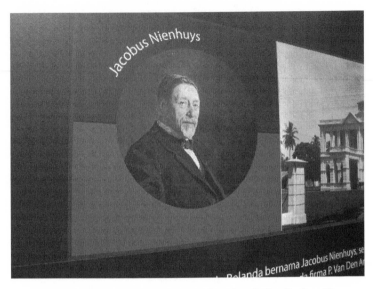

*Nienhuys, the tobacco pioneer and a founding father (indicted for
manslaughter and forced to flee Medan).*

case failed to repudiate the accusation. "He concluded that
no evidence had been found to contradict the story that
had been told," Breman wrote.[25] It was the first of many
coolie-related embarrassments the famed Deli Company
would face in the years to come. Nienhuys' speedy departure
paved the way for the entrance of the third "giant" of Deli,
my other great-great grandfather, Jacob Theodore Cremer.

Taming the Coolie Beast, written by Breman in 1987, published for the first time the details of an investigation into
the atrocities and abuses facilitated by the "Coolie Ordinance," a cynical piece of legislation pushed through by
the Dutch government in 1880 that essentially legalized
indentured labor, replete with penal clauses for workers who
refused to work or tried to escape the plantations to which
they were tied. Although applied throughout Indonesia,

(there was similar legislation in Malaya and Assam), the ordinance was in part the handiwork of my great-great grandfather Cremer, according to Breman.

"The government was needed to back up the private power of the planters," Breman told me in an interview. "Cremer hired a lawyer to draft the ordinance, and this man was a member of the Council of the Indies, so basically Cremer had him as a consultant and lobbyist." The ordinance allowed the plantation owners to hunt down fleeing laborers (usually with the assistance of cannibalistically inclined Bataks), beat them and send them to jail, after which they were returned to their jobs to fulfill three years of obligatory work. The legislation, and its abuses, prompted Dutch lawyer Johannes van den Brand to publish *The Millions of Deli* pamphlet in 1902, which shocked the Dutch public and prompted the government to launch an investigation into the alleged abuses. The investigation, conducted by Eurasian prosecutor J.I.T. Rhemrev, was carried out in 1903 and handed over to the Dutch government in early 1904. Rhemrev's full report was not made public until Breman broke the story in 1987.

It remains unclear whether the report by Rhemrev (whose name, like those of many Indonesian Eurasians was a Dutch surname spelled in reverse—Vermehr) was deliberately hidden from public scrutiny for more than a century or simply lost in the flotsam of colonial archives. "Although there was knowledge about the Rhemrev report, the report itself was never found," Breman told me. "I happened to find it and made it public in 1987." Breman, an international labor expert, chanced upon the report in the archives of the Dutch monarchy—Queen Wilhelmina was reigning at the time of the scandal. "The queen had access to all reports on colonial affairs, so in her state position it was sent to her and

My great-great grandfather Jacob Theodore Cremer.

then it got stuck or hidden away on purpose." The queen
may have had good reason to be concerned about the report.
The Dutch Trading Company, which had a 50-percent stake
in the Deli Company, was royally owned.

Cremer's thoughts on the coolie scandal, and his role
in the cover up of abuses committed under it, remain
unknown. But from his own writings one can decipher
a very cool, capitalistic character. In justification of the

Coolie Ordinance, Cremer wrote, "The only thing a worker owns is his labor power: on his side of it represents his collateral. If that is lost, then nothing is left, and the government therefore has no alternative but to confiscate it if the worker's proper fulfillment of the contract is to be guaranteed to some extent."[26]

Under the three-year contract laborers entered into with the tobacco plantations, they were charged for everything, including the tools they used, the seedlings they planted, their sleeping mats, pillows, the wooden planks of their beds and even the ledger in which the accounts of their work was kept. Women coolies had it worse than their male counterparts. "The women worked day and night: in the daytime with their hands and during the nights with their bodies," Breman wrote.[27] The laborers were encouraged to get into debt through licensed gambling and opium use on the plantations.

Cremer wrote cynically of the exploitative system, "By far the larger majority (of workers) do not bring their greatest defects with them, particularly opium smoking and gambling but learn them after their arrival in the colony which gave them plenty of opportunity to do so, not in order to meet an existing need but to create one, to the advantage of the government's treasury."[28] The government sold licenses to organize gambling and deal in opium to Chinese merchants as a form of taxation, and with the proceeds paid for the maintenance of the entire administration. "In 1878, profits from the sale of licenses brought in about as much money as all other forms of taxation... The costs of the civil service, of the judiciary and of the army could be defrayed entirely from the opium franchises, and were therefore paid for by the coolies themselves."[29]

Cremer was a staunch defender of the Coolie Ordinance during his term as minister of the colonies (1897 to 1901). When questioned in parliament by a socialist opposition party about reports of labor abuses in Deli, Cremer repeatedly denied the accusations. When portions of the Rhemrev report were leaked in 1904, essentially confirming the abysmal labor conditions outlined in *The Millions of Deli*, Cremer's public denials while serving as a minister were condemned. Once deemed a heroic pioneer of the Sumatran wilderness, he was thereafter stuck with the nickname "Coolie Cremer" for the remainder of his public career. Nonetheless, he went on to become a senator, president of the Dutch Trading Company and Dutch ambassador to Washington D.C. from 1918 to 1919 before retirement at his palatial Duin en Kruidberg villa in 1921.

The Coolie Ordinance, although modified in the wake of the Rhemrev report's findings, was not completely dropped until 1929, in response to trade sanctions imposed on Sumatran tobacco imports in the US market. Although not solely aimed at tobacco from Sumatra, the US government had passed legislation in 1929 that imposed bans on imported commodities that were produced with "unfree labor." "Of course, the tobacco lobby in Virginia was quite eager to enforce it," Breman said of the sanctions.

The coolie scandal also had a direct impact on the Janssen clan, who at that time had established themselves as a respectable nouveau riche family. Caroline Janssen, Peter W. Janssen's daughter, was so shocked by the revelations of *The Millions of Deli* pamphlet and the follow-up Rhemrev report that in 1903 she renounced her inheritance, which must have been considerable. "She was upset with the bad things happening in the Deli Company, so she gave my grandfather Carl Rehbock an order to spend her money for cultural purposes and so he did," said Frithiof Rehbock, Caroline's grandson. "All the money found a good place, but for us there was not much left. We had to earn our living which I think is good," he said. Frithiof, his sister Maryllia and brother Jaap all live in the Netherlands.

Jaap Rehbock is secretary of the P.W. Janssen Friesian Foundation, one of many charities set up by the first P.W. Janssen in Holland and his native Friesland. The organization owns about 1,500 acres of rural land, bought in 1885, which is now rented out to 36 cattle farms. The income from the Friesland farms still goes to charities. "We still support with the earnings from the Friesian lands many restorations, concerts, disabled and retarded people," Jaap informed me. In recent years, the Janssen Holland-based charities have come under some criticism for doing little for Indonesia, the source of the family fortune where there are many more needy people than in the Netherlands nowadays. "PWJ however did not realize that the money he received from Sumatra in fact should have been returned to those people (the former coolies) who made the Deli Company so extremely rich while they remained poor. But contrary to his colleagues Cremer and Nienhuys, PWJ at least tried to erect hundreds of institutions for the poor, disabled and retarded people, children and so on," Jaap said.

Despite his close links with the Coolie Ordinance, Cremer is still fondly remembered in Medan today, at least among the Indonesian business community, as one of the founders of the metropolis and its booming commerce. His statue now stands outside the original Deli Company headquarters on Jalan Tembaku Deli in northern Medan. In Holland too, Jacob Theodore Cremer has his admirers,

*A statue of Jacob Theodore Cremer outside the Deli Company head-
quarters in Medan, North Sumatra. The statue was put up in 1919
and taken down during the independence upheavals. It was later found
in the Public Works Department and returned to its original spot.*

some of whom are linked to another famed building—the Duin en Kruidberg, a countryside mansion in Santpoort, a popular seaside summer getaway for the wealthy families of Amsterdam for the past three centuries.

Cremer bought the Duin en Kruidberg villa in 1895, almost a decade after he had returned from Sumatra where he made his *Indisch Fortuin*. He would spend 205,000 guilders in the early 1900s on a major renovation of the mansion, whose previous owners included William of Orange, born in 1650 and King of England, as William III, until his death in 1702. "William III made Kruidberg as the location of his secret discussions to plan his expedition to England in 1688 to take the throne of his father-in-law, James II," notes a brochure on the mansion's history which was commissioned by the bank ABN AMRO, the current owner. William III successfully invaded England with a vast armada in 1688 and reigned jointly with his English wife Mary II until 1702. ABN AMRO converted Duin en Kruidberg into a modern conference center in 1997.

The mansion's structure remains much the same as it was after Cremer renovated the building and surrounding gardens in 1909. "Evidence of the life and tastes of Jacob Theodore Cremer (1847–1923) can be seen all around," says the ABN AMRO brochure on the building, compiled in collaboration with the Historical Society Velsen. Vestiges of Cremer's tropical career include murals in the central hall, of him driving "the first car to be driven in Sumatra—a Spijker," on a trip to Lake Toba. The car is depicted stuck in a shallow stream, Cremer fuming on the opposite bank. The next mural is of a party of Dutch ladies being carried in litters by bare-chested locals. Cremer also built a glasshouse at Duin en Kruidberg, where he grew his own tobacco, and in the garden he erected a statue of Mercury, the god of commerce. Frequent visitors to the estate included Prince Henry, husband of Queen Wilhelmina.

Cremer, from a patrician Gelderland-region family, in 1868 joined the royally-connected Nederlandsche Handel-Matschappij (NHM—Dutch Trading Company—a forerunner of ABN AMRO) and sailed to the Dutch East Indies when he was just 21 years old. After working for the NHM for more than three years in Batavia (the Dutch name of Jakarta) and Singapore, Cremer applied for the job as director of the Deli Company, which had been started by Nienhuys, Janssen and the NHM in North Sumatra in 1869. He was to prove an apt administrator. "With his organizational and commercial talents Cremer made the Deli Matschappij great and Deli Matschappij made him great ... a truly self-made man," the ABN AMRO blurb declares.

Cremer returned to Holland in 1883, ran for parliament and rose in domestic politics to become the minister of the colonies from 1897 to 1901, overseeing the affairs of North Sumatra among other colonies. In his spare time, he helped to set up the Colonial Institute (today's Royal Tropical Institute) and the Koninklijke Paketvaart Maatschappij (KPM—the shipping line that serviced the Dutch East Indies). He was appointed president of his first employer, the Dutch Trading Company, from 1907 to 1912, and Dutch ambassador to Washington D.C. from 1918 to 1919. He died in 1923, spending his last years at his palatial Duin en Kruidberg estate.

Duin en Kruidberg, a tourist attraction today, was not lived in by the Cremer family after World War II, when it was occupied by German army officers, who used the

The Duin en Kruidberg mansion in Santpoort.

immaculate gardens and grounds for target practice. Perhaps the Cremers wanted to move on. "Like many old castles and country estates, Duin en Kruidberg has its very own legend of a ghost," the ABN AMRO brochure says. "According to certain obscure sources, the spirit is a benign apparition, dressed in beige East Indian robe. ... A Javanese *kris*—perhaps originally owned by the ghost—is supposed to lie buried in the cellar of the house. To preserve good relations with the spirit, the *kris* (a tapered, ceremonial dagger used by the Malays, and believed to be alive) has never been moved," the brochure reads. Perhaps the ghost belongs to a Javanese coolie, a disgruntled sultan or is the shadow of Cremer's less-savory deeds in the Indies.

Cremer's success in turning the Deli Company into a highly profitable firm hinged upon his broader efforts to transform the Deli region into a "plantocracy," or a "state within a state," ruled by the big plantation owners. To be fair to the pioneers of Deli, it should be pointed out that one reason the plantations gained such power over their labor force and the local administration was because the state itself was so weak and undeveloped in North Sumatra. Sovereignty over the huge, jungle-covered island of Sumatra was a subject of dispute between the Dutch and the British after the invasion and occupation of Java by Thomas Stamford Raffles and 10,000 redcoats from 1811 to 1816.

Raffles committed several atrocities in Indonesia, including the bombardment of the palace of the Sultan of Yogyakarta in June 1811, something which the Dutch had never done in their then 200 years of colonial dominance over Java. He was also accused of clandestinely supporting the massacre of the Dutch community in Palenbang, Sumatra, allegedly to weaken the Dutch claim to the territory and also to help the British stake a claim to the nearby Palau Bangka tin mine. While he undermined the pseudo rule of the Javanese sultanate in Java forever, which the Dutch continued upon their return in 1816, Raffles' brief tenure also left Sumatra as fair game for both the Dutch and the British. The British, under Raffles, moved quickly to establish themselves across the Strait of Malacca in Penang and Singapore, two of the great trading posts for Southeast Asia.

The voyage of John Anderson, an employee of the East India Company's Penang office, to North Sumatra in 1822-23, makes it clear that the "Honourable Company" was interested in the abundant resources of the region, and worried about Dutch intentions to extend their rule over it. Anderson, in his *Journal of a Mission to the East Coast of Sumatra and Malayan Peninsula* (1823) took extensive notes on the natural abundance of the region, the alluvial soil that grew everything including tobacco, the cannibal-istic ways of the local Bataks and the slothfulness of both the Bataks and the Malays. "The excessive indolence of the natives, however, is a bar to all improvement. They gain a subsistence with little trouble or exertion, and devote the greater part of their time to sleep and idleness, smoking *meddat* (opium), etc," Anderson noted.[30]

Anderson, in his 1823 journal, also notes that the Dutch had made military inroads into Sumatra and were in the process of conquering the nearby sultanates of Padang and Riau. His main worry appears to have been the expected impact on British commerce, given the well-known propen-sity of the Dutch to impose a trade monopoly. "The rigid system of monopoly which is so generally introduced into their possessions, render it more imperative in us to pre-vent any unreasonable encroachment," Anderson wrote, in what might have been a hint at war-mongering.[31] Whatever his intentions, Britain did not take the bait, and Sumatra remained in Dutch hands.

In 1824, Britain signed an agreement with the Nether-lands to avoid interference on the Sumatran coast, which evolved into the Sumatra Treaty signed between the two governments in 1871, confirming that the government of the Straits Settlements, consisting of Penang, Singapore and some other more minor territories, waived all further interference in Sumatra.[32] This treaty came on the heels of the announcement in 1870 of Holland's "open door" policy in Indonesia, ending years of a state monopoly over agri-cultural extractions, in a bid to lure foreign investments to the colony. This incredibly liberal policy towards foreign investment was announced the year after the establishment of the Deli Company in Medan. It came seven years after the abolition of slavery in the Dutch East Indies, which happened in 1863, the same year US President Abraham Lincoln issued the Emancipation Proclamation, declaring all slaves in the Confederate States free. The US finally abolished slavery in 1865, two years after Indonesia. France ended slavery in Cambodia in 1884, and Thailand (then Siam) only abolished the practice in 1912.

The Dutch and other colonial powers in Southeast Asia were slower about abolishing indentured labor in their territories. This helps to explain why North Sumatra, with its open-door policy, became such a booming success, and why Southeast Asia enjoyed its first economic take-off. "Southeast Asian production sites gained appeal as political movements, and the abolition of slavery in parts of the Americas, made these locations less attractive depositories of Western capital," said Ann Laura Stoler, in her *Capitalism and Confrontation in Sumatra's Plantation Belt, 1870–1979*.[33]

North Sumatra was unique, as a production base, in its multinational flavor almost from the beginning of the commercial enclave. The population grew from an estimated 120,000 in 1880 to 420,000 in 1890, and to 1,200,000 in 1920. The rich alluvial soil drew the Dutch, the main investors in tobacco plantations, the British, who monopolized the tea estates, the Americans (such as Goodyear) in rubber plantations, and Belgians in palm oil. The plantations also attracted hundreds of young men from all over Europe seeking their fortunes in Deli, and tens of thousands of Chinese, Indian and Javanese laborers.

Working conditions, for both the low-level plantation managers and especially for the laborers, were brutal. Deli quickly earned a reputation for being the "Wild East," due to the lawlessness of the commercial area and the rough lifestyles of the *orang Deli*. The trials and tribulations of the young European men employed on the plantations in the early 1900s were well captured in *Tropic Fever–The Adventures of a Planter in Sumatra* written by the Hungarian author Ladislao Szekely, who worked on various plantations in North Sumatra from 1902 to 1918. He married Madelon Hermina Lulofs, another famed author of the anti-colonial ilk with her book *Rubber and Coolie*. But perhaps the most influential writer on government policy towards the colony was Johannes van den Brand, a Dutch lawyer based in Medan, who in 1902 published the booklet, *The Millions of Deli*, that would create a political scandal back in Holland.

The "coolie scandal" had an impact on the Senembah Company, which in the early 1900s was then under the directorship of Christian Wilhelm Janssen, Peter W. Janssen's eldest son. Unlike his father, Christian was a frequent visitor to North Sumatra, the land of the family fortune. His first trip there was in 1882, when Christian took a world tour at the age of 22 after completing his history studies in Geneva, Leipzig, Heidelberg and Strasbourg. In 1883, he returned to university in Strasbourg where he gained a PhD with his thesis on the *Dutch colonial economy in Batak-land Sumatra*. Christian returned to Sumatra in 1889 when he helped to set up the Senembah Company, with help from Cremer and Nienhuys, still directors of the Deli Company. But Christian seemed to have different ideas on how to manage the plantation, especially when it came to labor relations.

In a corporate history of the Senembah Maatschappij (1889–1939), Christian Janssen outlined the various reforms he had made to the plantation's management over the years.

For instance, he abolished the *tanggoen* system, under which an established *tandil* (laborer) would take over the debts of the new recruits, a system that led to many abuses, with gambling, opium addiction and store debts used to ensure the laborer could not leave. Also, money lending was prohibited. Christian displayed a philosophical side is his musings over the European management's relationship with the laborers. "When a human speaks to another human the dialogue is strongly affected by the inner attitude of the European towards the coolie. If he considers the coolie as a human being and he adjusts his orders, bringing them in line with what one can expect from a human being, and when his orders are shown respect, he can rely on the fact that the coolie will feel a bond and the coolie will be sympathetic towards him."

There was an open acknowledgement in Christian's writings that the Senembah Company's recruitment of Dutch agronomists was severely impacted by the coolie scandal after 1903. "For a while there was a tendency among graduates from the Wageningen (Dutch Agriculture University) to choose a Deli career, but this changed abruptly in 1903 when the public opinion was negatively influenced concerning the situation in Deli," he wrote. As a result, the Senembah hired mostly Swiss and German managers.

Attention was paid to improving medical facilities on the plantation, where malaria, beriberi, cholera and dysentery were rife, and German physicians with knowledge of tropical diseases were hired. Christian even pioneered providing education for the children of the workers, with limited success. One of the teachers Christian hired, a Ton Malahuk, would go on to become a revolutionary politician.

Breman, in his book *Taming the Coolie Beast*, is fairly kind to Christian Janssen and the Senembah. "A few planters distinguished themselves by treating their workers rather more leniently," he wrote.[34] "A director of the Senembah Company, C.W. Janssen, introduced a number of measures that ameliorated the miserable conditions under which the workers lived." In a telephone interview with me, Breman said, "That is where your ancestor Christian Janssen stands out. I wrote him up as lenient, and he certainly was." Breman, however, has little good to say about the Deli Company.

Over the decades, the Deli and Senembah companies would maintain close ties, as would the Cremer and Janssen families, culminating in what was widely viewed as a "business marriage" between Peter William Janssen II, my grandfather, and Henriette Jetske Cremer, my grandmother, on October 14, 1924. That marriage would end in divorce in 1951, when the two companies would also go their separate ways, with very different outcomes from nationalization in December 1957.

The Deli Company's diversification started during World War II, when Theo Cremer, a descendent of the famed Jacob Theodore Cremer, was dispatched to the United States with a shipment of tobacco, hurried out of Indonesia months before the Dutch colony was invaded by the Japanese Imperial Army and the Dutch forces, "after a valiant stand by the outclassed and outgunned Dutch air force and navy", surrendered on March 8, 1942.[35] Theo would sell the tobacco on the US market and set up a new company manufacturing machine-made cigar wrappers. In 1955, the Deli Company took control of the United States' American Sumatra Tobacco Corporation. Deli Maatschappij is still a listed company today, based in Rotterdam. While mainly involved in the furniture business, it still has small operations in tobacco.[36]

While Theo had left for America, my own grandfather, Peter W. Janssen II stayed behind in Sumatra to watch over the Senembah Company, a publicly listed firm in which the Janssen family had considerable holdings. He and his wife Henriette Jetske Cremer and their four children had moved to Sumatra in 1939, to avoid the mounting threat of a German invasion of Holland. Although they avoided the Germans, they did not escape the Japanese. The family would all be imprisoned in Japanese concentration camps during the war years.

CHAPTER 4

HARD TIME IN THE CAMPS

August Janssen, my father's elder brother, liked to write. In this, and in many other respects, he was unlike my father. August was a devout Christian Scientist who never drank, smoked or visited doctors—all of which go against the faith's beliefs. Herbert, my father was an alcoholic and heavy smoker. August took his studies seriously and became a teacher. My father found school tedious and expected to work for the family tobacco firm in Indonesia all his life, but President Sukarno thwarted him there. August was a faithful husband. My father was not. August died at the age of 76 in Denver, Colorado, surrounded by his loving family. My father died at the age of 39 in Grenada, in the Caribbean, divorced and alone.

My mother had flown down from Bronxville, New York, to be with my father on his deathbed. He died at 2.30 am on May 4, 1969. He had developed pneumonia after being hospitalized with a knife wound in the chest he had sustained in a drunken brawl with the younger brother of his then-girlfriend, Indira. Mom had tried to encourage him to keep fighting for breath. Dad had always been terrified of suffocation and would wake from nightmares panting for breath. His last words to her were, "It's too big a mess." A mess that started in Holland, with a privileged but peculiar upbringing, hardened by three years in Japanese concentration camps fighting for survival and becoming cynical.

The Janssen siblings—August, Mienske, Elizabeth and Herbert—spent their childhoods in the Gooilust mansion, near Amsterdam, raised by governesses, the most memorable of whom was Schwester Lizel, from Bavaria, Germany.

"German nannies were in demand by the upper classes in the Netherlands," August wrote in his book, *Not Guilty*, an autobiography. "They were tough. They exacted discipline, and August's parents needed a nanny desperately. They [the children] had become quite unmanageable. In no time, she had them singing Nazi songs. If the younger children did not behave themselves, they were kept under the [bath] water for a suitable amount of time," he wrote of Schwester Lizel.

Despite allowing this pro-Nazi upbringing, the Janssen parents—my Dutch grandfather, Peter William Janssen II, and Dutch granny, Henriette Jetske Cremer—felt it would be safer for the family to move to Indonesia as the German war machine began to threaten the Netherlands. In 1939, they boarded a ship for the Dutch East Indies, as Indonesia was then called. "We left from Ijmuiden, the closest harbor to the castle Duin en Kruidberg, where August's mother was born," August wrote. The mansion, once owned by Prince William of Orange, was bought by my great-grandfather, Jacob Theodore Cremer, in 1895.

*The Janssen children, August, Herbert, Elizabeth and Mienske
with their sadistic nanny Schwester Lizel of Bavaria.*

When the Janssen family arrived in Sumatra, Theo Cremer
(grandson of Jacob Theodore Cremer) was the managing
director of the Deli Company, headquartered in Medan,
while my grandfather Peter W. Janssen II (grandson of
Peter W. Janssen I) was managing director of the Senembah
Company, headquartered in the town of Tandjong Morawa,
outside Medan. The company had been founded by his uncle
Christian Janssen.

Theo Cremer and Peter Janssen II were third-generation
colonialists in Sumatra. They had both been born into fabulously rich families who had earned their fortunes using
coolie labor in the Deli plantation belt. In those days there
was no stigma of nepotism attached to family members
running the publicly owned Deli and Senembah companies, both listed on the Amsterdam stock exchange. "Those
two men had been guaranteed that they were going to be

the heads of the tobacco business, which had always been the wealth of the families," said Nancy Janssen-Currier, my mother.

Peter Janssen II would pay dearly for his hereditary post in the family empire during the war. When it became obvious in early 1942 that the Japanese were going to invade the Dutch East Indies, Peter and Theo decided that Theo should take a final shipment of tobacco to the USA to sell and use the proceeds to invest in the tobacco business there. Theo sailed in early 1942 to the USA where he eventually set up the Shade Grown Leaf Tobacco Company in Connecticut, in partnership with the US-based Homogenized Tobacco Leaf Co. He never invited Peter W. Janssen II to be a partner in the new company.

Peter Janssen II and the Janssen clan stayed behind in Indonesia to mind the Deli fort. In January 1942, my grandfather decided it would be safer to send his wife and the four children to Jakarta, then called Batavia, the capital of the Dutch East Indies, which was seen as less vulnerable to the pending Japanese invasion than Sumatra. August, in his diary, suspected my grandfather of another motive for shunting the family off to Java. "The other reason dad stayed behind was because of his girlfriend," August wrote.

The "girlfriend" was Lutske Nicolai, who would eventually become his stepmother after the war. "Papa went to the Social Club [in Medan] for dinner one night and Lutske saw him, and he saw Lutske," recalled my mother, who became good friends with Lutske. "It was the beginning of the end for both their marriages." At the time, Lutske was married to Constans Nicolai, a Dutch lawyer/civil servant who worked for the Council of Tropical Plantations in Medan.

My grandfather, whom I called Opa, and Lutske, whom I called Pooh, after "Winnie the Pooh", became an item in the tightly-knit Medan expatriate community some time before the war broke out. Lutske, her husband and two sons—Wouter and Adriaan—remained in Medan at the outset of the war. Wouter, who later became a successful agrarian expert/consultant, wrote his own memoir on the war years and his family's experiences in Sumatra during the Japanese occupation.

The government-in-exile of the Netherlands, which was invaded by Germany in May 1940, had declared war on Germany and Italy but not immediately on Japan. That changed after the bombing of Pearl Harbor on December 7, 1941, after which the Dutch East Indies were officially at war with Imperial Japan. "It was about February of 1942 that we began to see Japanese planes every day about 11 am in the morning," Wouter wrote in his account of the occupation. "Scout planes would be flying over the city, repeatedly passing over Polonia Airport which was close to our house. Everyone started constructing air raid shelters."

Japan's invasion of East and Southeast Asia unfolded quickly after Pearl Harbor, and within months their military had ousted the European colonial powers that had dominated the region for centuries. In rapid succession the Japanese army occupied Hong Kong, Kuching, Brunei, Vietnam, Thailand and Malaya. Singapore fell on February 15, 1942, leaving the Dutch East Indies wide open to invasion. On February 27, the Dutch navy lost the Battle of the Java Sea and by March 5, Jakarta was occupied. "The colonies were protected by a rather outdated navy and army which ran mostly on alcohol," August joked in his book. The Dutch officially surrendered on March 8, 1942, after less than a week of resistance. Medan was occupied by an army of Japanese cyclists on March 13.

"The occupation of Medan happened in an unspectacular fashion," Wouter wrote. "All of a sudden, groups of dirty-looking cyclists appeared on the streets. We finally realized that they were Japanese soldiers. Rifles were on their backs and their tunics were stained with urine as obviously they did not allow themselves time for relief. We were occupied." The invading cyclists had ridden all the way up to Medan from the tip of southern Sumatra. Wouter's father, Constans Nicolai, who had joined the Dutch army after mobilization was ordered in December 1941, became a prisoner of war. The family would not see him again until September 1945. Lutske, 8-year-old Wouter and 1-year-old Adriaan were sent to an internment camp in Sumatra.

There were approximately 250,000 Westerners living in the Dutch East Indies by 1942, of whom 220,000 were of Dutch descent, about half of whom were Eurasians of mixed Dutch-Indonesian blood. Some 170,000 of these expatriates were incarcerated in 358 civilian internment centers throughout the colony during the war years. Another 40,000 were made POWs, many of whom were put to work on war-related infrastructure projects.

Indonesians were not spared the war-time work detail. More than 4 million were conscripted into service for the Japanese effort, with Sukarno's support. Many died from disease and malnourishment. They were forced to work alongside Dutch and Allied POWs on the Pakanbaru Railway project, laying a 220-kilometer track through the Sumatran jungle, and even on the Death Railway, a 265-kilometer line built in 12 months through the jungles of Kanchanaburi province, Thailand, and the Mon State,

Burma, which claimed the lives of 13,000 Western POWs and another 70,000 Asians.

The camps were a life-changing experience for the Janssen clan, the pampered progeny of three generations of colonial wealth. "In the War, August saw an opportunity to become a normal human being," August Janssen wrote in his autobiography. The swift Japanese occupation of Jakarta had separated the family, with Peter Janssen II stranded in Medan while his wife and children were forced to fend for themselves in Jakarta.

It was a particularly challenging time for Jetske Janssen, the delicate scion of the fabulously wealthy Cremer family. "Mrs. Janssen had arrived at her Rubicon. In a short time, most of her cash had disappeared," August wrote of his mother. "Papa had a breakdown."

Jetske, poorly prepared for marriage and motherhood, was even less ready for the trials and tribulations that lay ahead in the internment camps. "Granny was unprepared to be a protector of anybody," said my mother. "It's just amazing that she lived through it herself, because she had no skills whatsoever. She hadn't even combed her own hair. She had no idea how to start a campfire and put on a little soup, so Mienske [her eldest daughter] was the one who did all the work. And she resented it terribly that Jetske was so weak."

Despite her lack of worldly experience, Jetske did demonstrate some moral fiber, given her privileged position prior to the occupation. "Just before the Japanese invaded, I had an offer from the representative of the KNILM (Royal Dutch Indies Airline Company) to fly me and my children out to Australia. I declined the offer. Now I have great doubts that it was the right decision," Jetske wrote in a letter discovered by her son August after the war. "Instead she took on her shoulders to help comfort or at least to help save the lives of many of the women and children who had followed her to Java. She sold most of her jewelry, except for one large diamond which she always wore around her neck and which was worth at least $5,000. *Kempeitai* [Japanese military police] picked Mama up and beat her up. They took her necklace," August wrote.

The Janssens were allowed to live in their rented house in Jakarta for several months after the Dutch surrender, while the Japanese occupation forces decided what to do with the European and Eurasian communities. Eventually, most would be sent to "internment" camps, as the concentration camps were called. Eventually, the Janssen boys—August and Herbert—were sent to internment camps for men while Jetske, Mienske and Elizabeth were dispatched to a camp for women. Conditions in the camps went from bad to worse as the war went on, and more and more food and medicine were requisitioned for the occupying Japanese forces and their comrades in far-flung battlefields such as Papua and Borneo.

August would be interned in a succession of camps in Java, starting with the Bondowoso concentration camp, which was run by the Indonesian police rather than the Japanese. "The worst thing about the place was there was nothing to do but eat and sleep," he wrote. After Bondowoso he was moved to Tangerang, Tana Tanggi and Tjimahi camps, where the previously flippant young man—August was 18 years old at the time—had an epiphany that led him to study Christian Science, a religion he took seriously his whole life. "For the first time in Janssen's life, he is determined to learn something," he wrote. In order to better understand Mary Baker Eddy's belabored *Science and Health with Keys*

Henriette Jetske Cremer, my Dutch grandmother and descendant of Jacob Theodore Cremer, a founder of the Deli Company in Medan, North Sumatra.

to the Scriptures, August decides to improve his English first. On October 11, 1944, he started to keep a diary. At Tjimahi camp, with 14,000 inmates, the average death rate was about 10 a day, he claimed. The greatest death toll in the camps was among the elderly and the very young.

On November 30, 1944, the Janssen brothers were reunited by a lucky coincidence that no doubt saved my father's life. August recorded the chance reunion with his younger brother, who because of his age had initially been living in the women's camp with his mother and sisters for their first two years of incarceration. "Herbert is small for his age. His group arrived by train at Tjimahi. He didn't like the group he was in, so he walked over to another one. This one was moved to Tjimahi." Big brother August and his friend "Rubens" shared their meagre food rations with Herbert, who was sickly and verging on starvation. "On January 28 [1945], it is reported that Herbert is gaining weight and the rest of us stayed at AP (an abbreviation for *Amsterdams Peil*, used in Europe as a measure of water levels)" August wrote. By April, Herbert had a voracious appetite and had been restored to good health.

After the USAAF dropped atomic bombs on Hiroshima on August 6, 1945 and Nagasaki on August 9, Japan finally announced its intention to surrender on August 15. With the defeat, conditions improved in the camps and there was finally a freer flow of information after three years of news blackouts and no communications with relatives.

There was bad news for the Janssen brothers. "A friend of mine tells me that Elizabeth, my little sister, has died in the women's camp. Herbert cries most of the night," wrote August. The loss of Elizabeth, his beloved sibling, was a terrible blow for my father which he probably never got over.

My mother would attribute his love for her as a substitute for his devotion to his lost sister.

On September 4, 1945, the Janssen brothers crawled through a hole in the fence at Tjimahi camp and somehow made their way to Jakarta. August was unclear how this feat was carried off in his diary, although family legend has it that they took a train. They found their way back to the rented house on Madiun Road which they had occupied before the war and were reunited with Mama and Mienske, and eventually Papa. "After a week or so in the house on Madiun Road, Peter W. Janssen, the dad, suddenly shows up," wrote August. "The first one he saw was his daughter, Mienske. He thought she was his wife. Mienske straightened him out in a hurry. By this time, the Indonesians had started to fight for their independence. Accordingly, the Janssen family escaped to Singapore on an army airplane." They put up at the Raffles Hotel, the best establishment in town. It's nice to have money.

Having money did not help my Opa much during the Japanese occupation of Sumatra. He was singled out for months of torture and solitary confinement in what appeared to be efforts to extract, not military secrets, but where he had hidden his cash. He had none. Theo Cremer had departed with the last shipment of tobacco and Peter Janssen II was left holding a bag of nothing. Opa never talked about his experiences during the war, but Lutske told me that he was forced to stand for hours without a bathroom break. "You know your grandfather. He hated to mess himself. He was so humiliated," she recounted to my sister and me when we were children.

After his harsh treatment by the Japanese, Opa was sent to the internment camps in North Sumatra and ended up

in Si Rengo Rengo, one of the most notorious. As food supplies shrank at the end of the war, the Japanese concentrated
the men prisoners at Si Rengo Rengo and the women at
Aek Panimke camps in North Sumatra. By the time they
arrived in Si Rengo Rengo most of the inhabitants were
in bad shape already. Of the 1,250 prisoners who entered
the camp, only 750 survived the 10-month incarceration.
Among them was Wouter Nicolai. Peter Janssen II acted
as a guardian for the young Wouter, although given the
severe food and medicine shortages they all suffered, there
was not much he could do.

Prior to Si Rengo Rengo, Wouter spent about two years
in various camps with his mother, Lutske, and younger
brother, Adriaan. Lutske shone in the tough camp environment, where she demonstrated a flair for survival. "My
mother started to get involved in the dangerous activity of
selling items of jewelry for herself and others and to use
the proceeds to buy food," Wouter recalled in his autobiography. "She was arrested and held for days in confinement
with beatings and no food." When Wouter turned 11 he
was forced to leave the women's camp and was moved to
Si Rengo Rengo. Lutske gave him a tin of Quaker Oats
she had hoarded and told him to only open it when he
became desperate for food. Wouter would hold on to the
treasure from his mother for 10 months, refusing to open
it even though he was on the verge of starvation. Instead
of Quaker Oats, the Americans saved him.

"None of us who were in Japanese concentration camps
will ever question the wisdom of President Harry Truman
in deciding to go ahead and drop bombs on Hiroshima and
Nagasaki," Wouter wrote. "Had the war lasted another few
months many of us, me included, would not have survived.

We were literally at death's door." After 10 months in Si Rengo Rengo, nearly 12 years old, Wouter weighed 20 kilograms. "I had no hair, no fingernails and no toenails," he wrote. Incredibly, he still had the tin of Quaker Oats, uneaten.

Wouter was reunited with his mother and younger brother, but their troubles were not over. "Immediately upon the capitulation by the Japanese, the Indonesians declared on August 17, 1945, their independence from the Netherlands and started arming themselves with weapons and ammunition from the Japanese army. We were confined to camps but ironically the Japanese were now protecting us," Lutske wrote in a letter to her parents saved by Wouter. She had no love for her new protectors. "Never, never will you understand how we were treated by the Japanese yellow animals. One thing I can tell you …The Japanese are not human. They treat, especially the women, with Oriental sadism. We are presently in the jungle located about 300 kilometers from Medan. I was always lucky, had no fear and am quite handy. And with that we have to start rebuilding."

The Nicolai family were lucky in that they lost no one in the camps or the war. Even their father, who had been sent to work on the notorious Death Railway in Thailand, miraculously survived. He was eventually dispatched to the remaining camps in North Sumatra. He was one of three POW survivors sent to find their families in the camps. Wouter recounted their reunion. "Then my mother let out a loud, a very loud, scream. One of the men was her husband, my father." But the family ordeal was not over. On their way from the camp to Medan their train was attacked by Indonesian "freedom fighters," leaving them stuck in the sweltering train cars for two days before they could continue their journey. "In mid-December our family was put on notice for repatriation to the Netherlands on the Dutch-American vessel Noordam. It would carry 2,000 Dutch men, women and children back to their homeland," wrote Wouter. Again, the Nicolais were lucky to get out alive.

Many Dutch and Eurasians died in the so-called *Bersiap* (get ready) period of terror, following Sukarno's announcement of independence and the unleashing of the *permuda* or young freedom fighters. The Eurasian community resulting from colonialism was a particular target of the terror. Many of the estimated 160,000 Eurasians were interned along with the Dutch in the Japanese camps during the war. Hated for their mixed heritage and former privileged status under Dutch rule when Eurasians dominated the civil service, thousands were killed during the "Permuda Terror" that lasted from August to December 1945, before order was finally restored by Allied forces. The *permuda* roamed the countryside armed with machetes and spears. They attacked the bands of Dutch and Indos who had survived the concentration camps and were trying to make their way to safety. Unknown thousands were raped and slain in the aftermath of the horrors of the camps.

"Two revolutions were taking place—the military one between the Netherlands and the new Republic of Indonesia, and the social one between native islanders and their former rulers," Ilse Evelin Veere Smit wrote in her chilling and beautifully crafted account of her Eurasian family's ordeal first in the camps and later on their trek through Java to safety during the *Bersiap* period. *Bersiap* was one of the slogans shouted by the *permuda* gangs. The Dutch and Indo survivors of the concentration camps were unprepared for the savage attacks on them after the Japanese surrender.

"They hate you mixed bloods even more than they hate the Hollanders," an old Indonesian woman explained to the Veere family, after taking them in and giving them food and shelter for a night during their harrowing escape from a concentration camp in East Java. "These young hot bloods are angry at you because you turned against us and married the Dutch to help them make slaves out of your own people."

My Dutch relatives never spoke much about the occupation or the *Bersiap* period, deciding it was better to forget past unpleasantness. Much seems to have gone unsaid, including what they no doubt endured under the Japanese. Other Dutch memoirs of the period are more explicit. Rape was commonplace. "Because the Japs could not get enough Indonesian prostitutes and women to satisfy their needs, the controller was ordered by the Japanese to go to the internment camps and ask for Dutch, American and English women who would give themselves as prostitutes for the Japs. The controller found some German women and ordered them to the barracks," wrote Matt Gavin, in his book *Two to Be Remembered* based on the recollections of Ernest Hubert-Flissinger. He was the son of a Dutch businessman who spent his youth in Java, witnessed the Japanese invasion and the *Bersiap* period before migrating to the USA. "And rape was the thing. I saw women, many mothers pregnant, being raped in the streets in open sight of the police. It is hard to fathom the absolute reversal of fortunes the Indo-Europeans had suffered. In just a few months they had gone from elite to outcasts." Of the *Bersiap* period, Gavin wrote, "The natives rampaged through the towns on the islands of Java and Sumatra, killing thousands upon thousands of Europeans. Heads and genitals were cut off."

Ilse Evelin Veere Smit, in her book *End the Silence*, co-authored by Dorothy Reed, hints at the abuse her own Eurasian mother was subject to at Halmasheira camp in Semarang, Java. "My mother was assigned to a select group that worked outside the gates. She said she worked in the rice fields but I never, before or after the internment, saw any evidence of rice fields near Camp Halmasheira. It was a mystery never solved. Her mother died on August 17, 1945, two days after the surrender on August 15, she wrote. "All my life I have been told I must put the memories behind me but the memories are still vivid," she said, in an introduction to the book. I wish my Dutch relatives had been similarly forthcoming about their own experiences, but these are now lost.

In Singapore, at Raffles Hotel, my father kept his own diary for a few months before the family moved to the USA where he would go to a Christian Science boarding school and meet my mother. On November 6, he wrote, "Today there arrived 3,000 women from Java. The locals turned angry against the Europeans. They murder almost every European they can get their hands on. It's about time for the women and children to be evacuated." And on November 11, "It's a tremendous mess in Java. It is worse in Batavia, where you get killed just walking in the streets." And on November 18, "Changi is a big camp of approximately 4,000 Dutch people. A lot of tents." Changi had been a large POW camp run by the Japanese during World War II.

The wealthy Janssen family, safe in the Raffles Hotel, had their own traumas to deal with. On November 30, my father wrote, "Dad had a malaria attack again." And on his own birthday on December 4, "Today is my birthday. I am 15 now. Dad gave me a shockproof and waterproof watch. When I lay in bed last night I thought about my last birthday in the camp and how grateful I was for some extra food. I'll try to stay that grateful because I have much more reason to be grateful now."

Shortly thereafter, the Janssens departed for the USA on a cruise liner, arriving in New York on February 24, 1946. Herb would enter Principia high school where he would meet Nancy Ruth DeGarmo, his future wife, and take her back to Indonesia, where he had spent three years of his youth in Japanese concentration camps, a traumatizing experience that no doubt contributed to the darker, self-destructive aspects of his character which were to blossom in yet another tropical paradise—the island of Grenada in the West Indies.

CHAPTER 5

GOING TO GRENADA—CARIBBEAN HIDE-AWAY

After being expelled from Indonesia in 1957, the Janssen clan was at a loose end, especially my mother and father. My grandfather Peter W. Janssen II and his wife Lutske moved back to Holland, where they resided first in a rented mansion in Gooilust, a historical site. My sister and I accompanied our grandparents on the flight out of Singapore—after again staying at the Raffles Hotel—in January 1958 and were shortly afterwards joined by our parents.

The Janssens were not the only refugees arriving in the Netherlands from the former Dutch East Indies, now very much the new independent archipelago nation of Indonesia. An estimated 46,000 Dutch nationals were expelled from Indonesia in December 1957, and perhaps more than 100,000 Eurasians joined them in the exodus. The Dutch economy was hardly booming in 1958, and political attention was shifting away from Asia towards Europe and the newly launched European Economic Community (1957). The old colonialists were seen as an unwanted anachronism.

"The Dutch people were not impressed by old wealth anymore. They had had their fill of rich people who had made mistakes," my mother recalled of the adaptation challenges faced by her father-in-law Peter W. Janssen II and Lutske, who was from humbler background than his first wife Henriette Jetske Cremer. "Everything had changed for the rich people, and Lutske was very helpful for Papa because she was someone who had not always lived in elegance. Although Lutske liked to be rich, she liked sounding poor." Lutske helped Opa downsize, moving them out of the Gooilust mansion into a more modest villa in Blaricum. Eventually, they would migrate to a warmer and, initially, a more welcoming environment.

My father, a high school graduate with several years of experience as a tobacco plantation manager, did not find himself in big demand in Holland. There was no family business to offer him a job, although the family-founded Deli Company survived for generations, diversifying into many non-tobacco related activities such as construction materials and furniture making. "Papa had no idea what to do with Herbert to help him," my mother recalled. "I always felt so sorry for Herbert. He hadn't the strength to take the lead and he was confused as to what to do now. And, of course, that was true just about everybody."

After a few months of dithering, my father and mother decided to try their luck in the land of opportunity, the USA. Uncle Theo Cremer, who was doing well for himself in Connecticut with the Shade Leaf Tobacco Company he had set up on the proceeds from selling the last shipment of Sumatra tobacco in 1942, initially offered my father a job, "but it never worked out," my mother recalled. "Part of the time we were at my mother's and dad's, but they were going through a hard time because my father's business had fallen through. I felt very guilty about being on their doorstep," she said.

My father decided to move the family to New Orleans, where the weather was less chilly. "We went to New Orleans, for no reason at all other than he liked the atmosphere," my mother said. In New Orleans my father got a job working at a Buster Brown factory (once famous for their underwear products, the logo features a fay looking dude with his pooch, Buster) that happened to be run by a Christian Scientist. This was a pleasant time for my mother and her marriage. "I was extremely happy, and he (Herbert) seemed happy with me."

Our family spent less than three years in New Orleans. My first childhood memories are of attending a Mardi Gras carnival where I managed to catch some free candies. My father went off to work every day, sometimes bringing back free Buster Brown underwear for us. We lived simply and "ordinarily" in a rented house, played on the sidewalks with my first friend Raymond, who was autistic and whose speech was incomprehensible to everyone else but me and eventually entered kindergarten, well on our way to becoming good little Americans. But the American dream was not to last.

"Then Papa and Lutske came for a visit and said, 'This job is nothing. We're going to South America to do this and that,' and we ended up in Grenada," my mother recalled. Pooh and Opa, fed up with the gloomy weather in the Netherlands and the lack of affordable servants there, decided to take a world cruise in 1960-61, looking for an alternative retirement home, preferably somewhere warm and hospitable. They ended up in Grenada, a British colony in the West Indies, surrounded by the Caribbean.

When they cruised into the port of St. George's, Grenada's capital, they thought they had discovered paradise on Earth and decided to move there, according to Pooh's telling of the tale which we heard as children. Baresford Wilcox, a British architect and developer, also had something to do with the decision. Bares—as he was known to us—and his talented Norwegian architect wife, Kari, had purchased an entire peninsula on the northern tip of Grenada called Westerhall Point which they wanted to transform into an exclusive housing development for rich white people.

The only problem was they had not found any rich white people yet to invest in a property there. Enter the picture, Peter W. Janssen II. Opa bought a house and prime piece of land on Westerhall Point with access to his own private beach and a beautiful view of the ocean. Kari Wilcox, who did not believe in glass windows, designed an unusual one-story construction which was open to the elements, including the mosquitoes and other insects. But the Janssens had plenty of experience with tropical insects, having survived Indonesia and three years in the camps.

Bares and Kari Wilcox were a gifted, hard-working couple. They had practiced as architects in Sweden in the 1950s before moving to Venezuela to try their luck in that South American dictatorship that was experiencing a bit of a building boom after the discovery of oil offshore. One of Kari's uncles was a captain on a cargo ship and gave the entire family, including three children—Trina, Neil and Colin—a free ride to Caracas, Venezuela's steamy capital. They decided to stay. "That was with no savings, three children under five years old, not speaking the language and having no contacts," said Colin, the youngest son and still a good friend of the Janssen family.

After three years of barely making ends meet in Caracas, the Wilcoxes took a family vacation in Grenada, and decided to move there. They discovered Westerhall Point, which was mostly a sugar plantation then, and bought the entire peninsula in 1958, after securing a personal loan from Bares' father and a bank overdraft. "They put much emphasis on landscaping, planting over 70,000 scrubs and trees," Colin said. They also built a paved road around the peninsula. The Wilcoxes built three houses on spec and sold one house and two plots of land to Opa. "The Opa sale would have been quite significant for my parents, not only because it was a house sale but because they bought the land next door to them as well at a time when funds were quite critical," he said. Opa would claim he bought the additional plot to bail Bares out at a time when the Westerhall Point project was struggling.

Westerhall remains today one of the most upmarket, best designed, greenest housing developments in Grenada which is certainly one of the most naturally beautiful islands in the West Indies. Unlike nearby Barbados and Trinidad, which are flat coral-formed islands, Grenada is the offspring of a volcano and is therefore mountainous, albeit with only one real mountain—the Grand Egang (Big Pond)—which has an extinct volcano with a giant pool at its center. There are waterfalls on the mountain and hence plenty of fresh water for the islanders.

Around the island, which is about 7 by 12 miles, are many beaches, including some stunning black-sand ones and more common white-sand ones such as the Grand Anse (Big Sand) which is the most popular among tourists and

Opa's veranda with a sea view in Westerhall Point,
Grenada, West Indies.

Our house, hillside view, in Westerhall Point, Grenada,
West Indies.

the cruise boats. The island boasts a population of about 100,000. The mean temperature is 80 degrees Fahrenheit and there is nearly always a pleasant tropical breeze blowing, which, during hurricane season, can turn into a mighty breeze indeed.

The only drawback to Grenada, besides the hurricanes, is that there is not much to do there other than watch the magnificent sunsets and drink whisky and rum. My grandparents, after buying their posh, open-air bungalow by the sea, found that they were getting bored. It was around this time that they visited my parents in New Orleans and decided that my father's job at Buster Brown underwear factory "was nothing" and we all deserved more from life.

The Calypso call to my father was made, and he listened to it, and unlike the wily Odysseus he never escaped it. We packed up our bags, said goodbye to our American friends in New Orleans, and headed out for a new tropical paradise, this time in the West Indies instead of the Dutch East Indies. The lotus eaters—my parents—were on the road again.

My grandfather was initially interested in starting a tobacco plantation in Grenada, but dropped the project once he discovered that Grenadians, most of them descendants of African slaves, were not tempted by back-breaking labor for poor wages. The dream, however, was not unrealistic. There are striking similarities between Grenada and North Sumatra, including rich volcanic soil and plenty of sunshine—two of the necessary ingredients for tobacco to thrive. Grenada was also no stranger to colonization.

Grenada was discovered by Christopher Columbus in 1498 on his third voyage to the Americas. He dubbed the island La Concepcion. It was later changed by a Spanish mapmaker in 1523 to Granada, after Granada, Spain. The island was then under the control of the Carib Indians, a fierce tribe that did not welcome immigrants. They called the island Camerhogue. The Spaniards didn't stick around for long in Concepcion/Camerhogue thanks to the hostile reception from the natives. French "settlers" started to arrive on the island in 1650 and renamed the place La Grenade, because it looks like a grenade—a big lump of metal in the ocean. The French massacred the Carib Indians between 1651 and 1654 as part of the "settlement" process, forcing the last remnants of the tribe to jump off a cliff—since called Leapers' Hill, appropriately—in a tragic example of auto-genocide. In 1763, the island was ceded to Britain as part of the Treaty of Paris. The British quickly rechristened their new conquest "Grenada," a name and spelling that finally stuck.[37]

Under British rule Grenada joined the plantation economy, growing mainly sugarcane and tobacco. Since there were no indigenous inhabitants, thanks to the French handiwork with the Carib Indians, slaves were imported from Africa. The same phenomenon was occurring in the rest of the West Indies in other British colonies such as Barbados, and Trinidad and Tobago, which were almost exclusively dedicated to sugar-cane estates and were far more lucrative for the colonialists than Grenada. Unlike, Trinidad and Barbados, however, Grenada proved to be an ideal place for growing tobacco, perhaps because of the rich volcanic soil.

"Tobacco grown in Grenada at the time was said to be of such superior quality that it realized double and triple the price of that grown in the other islands," wrote George Brizan, in his book *Grenada - Island of Conflict*.[38] So, my grandfather's aspirations for creating a new North Sumatra were not wholly fanciful, except for the lack of "coolie labor". While Grenada was always a relatively small revenue earner for Britain, it was hardly an insignificant one. In 1773, exports from Grenada were worth eight times those from Canada.[39] In the late 18th century the West Indies were for Britain the equivalent of the Dutch East Indies while the new colonies in North America such as Virginia and New York were relative under-performers.

Slavery was a fact of life in the Caribbean until July 31, 1838, when it was abolished after sustaining the region's sugar plantations for 276 years. The institution had sparked several slave uprisings including the Feron Revolution in Grenada (1795–96), that claimed up to 7,000 lives. Ironically, it was the rise of other sources of sugar-cane, such as the Philippines and Indonesia in Southeast Asia, that ultimately undermined the sugar barons of the Caribbean. Their production costs had soared and their exports were no longer competitive especially after Britain dropped protective tariffs on other sources of sugar. Without its dominance in the sugar trade, the West Indies went into slow decline. Their populations of African descent faced dismal employment prospects. Grenada was no exception although its economy was bolstered somewhat by a new export—nutmeg.

Indonesia had another unique connection to Grenada through the nutmeg industry. Nutmeg is only indigenous to the Banda Islands on the eastern extremity of the Indonesian archipelago. The Dutch were initially drawn to Indonesia in 1603 by the nutmeg trade, which was then dominated by Portugal. At the time nutmeg, seen as a panacea in Europe, was worth its weight in gold. The Dutch savagely conquered Banda and thereafter Java, establishing a trading post in

Batavia (now Jakarta) for the sake of securing the lucrative nutmeg trade which they monopolized for decades, banning the export of the nutmeg plant outside of Banda.

This changed in 1811, when Sir Stamford Raffles successfully launched an invasion of Java and conquered the defending Dutch forces. Raffles committed several atrocities in the course of his short reign over Indonesia, including the raid and demolition of the Sultan's Palace in Yogyakarta and provoking a massacre of Dutch inhabitants in Palembang, Sumatra.[40] Raffles also started exporting nutmeg plants to other British colonies such as India. Although India is now one of the leading exporters of nutmeg, which has lost its "weight in gold" value, the quality does not compare with that of Indonesian or Grenadian nutmeg.

The nutmeg plant was first introduced to Grenada in 1843 by British citizen Frank Gurney. Commercial-scale cultivation did not take off until 1860, coinciding with the decline of sugar production on the island as its chief cash crop. By 1910, Grenada accounted for 14% of world nutmeg exports, rising to 33% in 1918.[41] The nutmeg crop, primarily in the mountainous region, was pretty much wiped out by Hurricane Janet in 1955, but it was replanted and by 1975 nutmeg was the island's leading industry.

My family arrived in Grenada in mid-1962, by which time Opa had already given up on the tobacco plantation scheme and, as he knew nothing about nutmeg, that was not an option either. But he did agree to lend Herbert money to start a construction business, something they both knew nothing about. Lacking the rudimentary knowledge of putting up houses, my father found a local business partner—Mr Blanco, who would turn out to be a crook. A new phase of the Janssen family history had begun.

When we arrived on Westerhall Point we already had designated friends—part of the pitch Opa and Pooh had made to persuade my mother that Grenada was a perfect place to raise a young family. Our arrival was a watershed of sorts for the Wilcox children—Trina, Neil and Colin. "We all went over to Lutske's house to meet you and you had presents for us; I got a Native American costume which I loved, and changed into immediately," Colin recalled. "There were no other children locally, so it was a special day for us."

For schooling there was Mr Sandler, an elderly gentleman who lived in a modest house on Westerhall Point hill. It was quite a walk to his place, in the equatorial sun. The Sandler school didn't last long. He left the island shortly after his wife left him for another man. For a few months, my mother attempted to home-school us, but this proved a disaster, perhaps because Mom was so smart and we were so un-smart. We eventually ended up at West Morland, a private grammar school in St. George's run by an eccentric British teacher, Barrell Ball. Ms. Ball was a firm believer in the benefits of corporal punishment and would skip with glee between the desks to slap you on the palm with her ruler should you blunder in class. Josie and I lived in perpetual terror of prompting the Ms. Ball skip.

We lived on Westerhall Point in a modest, one-story house built by the Wilcoxes and paid for by Opa. It was on a slight rise and had a nice view of Westerhall Bay, but no private beach, unlike Opa's house. There were three bedrooms, a porch where we would eat and the kitchen and servant's room, where our beloved maid—Josephine—resided. Josephine was always grumpy and liked to say, "Don't vex me, child," when we were vexing.

Josie E. Janssen, with her beloved Raggedy Ann, and
Peter W. Janssen III, with cap.

The Wilcox children were our only friends on Westerhall because they were the only other children there. They were pleasant, at first, but proved a bit oppressive and arrogant in the longer run. Their father, Bares, was a more successful builder than our father, and since they were British they looked down on our materialistic American culture, except during Christmas when we got so many more presents from the Sears catalogue and our American grandparents than they did.

The Wilcox parents had struggled to make a success of Westerhall Point, whereas our family never really had to worry because Opa had money and would always bail us out if Herbert failed. My father despised Bares, primarily because he was more successful than he was. He would stop our car in front of a donkey on the road and say, "Hi Bares, what are you doing here?" The mutual hatred didn't do much for my status in the Wilcox family. Once I was playing with Neil and Colin and Neil called me "stupid." Bares came out of his room and reprimanded Neil's American pronunciation. 'It's not 'stoopid.' It's 'styoopid,'" he elucidated. Thank you, Mr Wilcox.

But the Wilcox children have fond memories of our family, especially of my mother who was always nice and fair with them, unlike my father who could be cruel and nasty to the "boys" because he disliked Bares. The Wilcox children would come over every Sunday to attend Sunday school, my mother's doomed attempt at instilling religion in us. Colin did a composition for a writing class he attended in Britain, years later, which described the Sunday sessions which I include as an appendix because it captures some of the charm of our Grenadian lifestyle and also provides a glimpse of my mother's personality (see *"The Teacher by Colin Wilcox"* on page 129).

Peter W. Janssen III (aged about 7), on the tropical island paradise of Grenada, West Indies.

Rex, our promised pet, in Grenada, West Indies.

My parents' marriage started to fall apart. Dad began to drink a lot. There was not much else to do. Every weekend we would go to the Tennis Club, on the hill above St. George's, and Herbert and Nancy would play tennis with Robbin and Jean Rennick, a Grenadian couple who were their two best friends. The Rennicks were an influential local family that had migrated to Grenada from Barbados. They were big players in the nutmeg industry, which is managed by a cooperative between the landholders and the growers. Robbin was handsome, athletic, humorous and liked his rum. My father was an adequate athlete and also liked his rum, along with his whisky, beer and whatever else was available. Nancy, still a good Christian Scientist, drank a lot of Coca-Cola in Grenada.

The crash finally came in April 1966, when my mother was 34 years old. It started at the Nutmeg, a popular restaurant/bar in St. George's where my parents were hanging out with the Rennicks after a weekend tennis match. After four years of hanging out with the Rennicks in Grenada, Nancy had developed a crush on Robbin which Herbert had become aware of. "He was always fooling around but he did not want me to be attracted to anyone," Nancy recalled, in an interview with her niece Molly Saldo, years later.

Herbert had been drinking heavily and when they were leaving the Nutmeg, which had a very narrow entrance, he ran in to a car trying to come in. Instead of backing up, he rammed the incoming car and almost pushed it into the harbor. Nancy ran back inside the Nutmeg and got Robbin to come down and calm Herbert down. "Herbert was sitting in the car, and the other car had decided to back off," Nancy said. "We started to drive away and he started hitting me. When we got outside St. George's he said, 'Get out of the car.' I got out in my tennis dress with my tennis racket and I decided to walk to Jean Rennick's house and spend the night there. It was pitch black and I passed two big black guys and they said, 'Oooo. She mad.' And I said, 'Yes. I mad.' And they didn't bother me. But Herbert relented and came back and picked me up, but I thought, 'This marriage is ruined.'"

Back in Westerhall Point, Nancy left her home to walk to the house of the LeMays, an American couple who were our neighbors and friends, which was perched on a cliff. Herb picked her up before she could get there (a walk of well over a mile), but it didn't save the marriage. "I was suicidal at that point and I realized that I was a psychological mess and I needed to get off the island and I had to get the kids out of there," Nancy said.

Shortly after that, we got on a plane and flew to America, destined for Red Bank, New Jersey, where we moved into my American grandparents' house on the southern bank of the Navesink River. Grandad DeGarmo was kind to us, trying to instill American values into us via softball lessons in their backyard. After Josie knocked a softball through their terraced porch's window, he nicknamed her "Slugger Joe." I was a less impressive softball player and earned no such nickname.

Josie and I, after four years in the Caribbean, were like island rubes with the sand still between our toes. We were far behind in our schooling, even by American standards. We went to summer school in Red Bank, while Mom applied to return to Sarah Lawrence College and finish her musicology degree, which had been interrupted by marriage, Indonesia and then the West Indies. She was accepted, and thus confirmed her old dean's prophecy that "you'll be back."

When the school term began in the autumn of 1966, we moved to Bronxville, New York, renting a small, cheap apartment close to Sarah Lawrence College. Mom became a college girl again, at age 34, and Josie and I were enrolled in Daycroft, a Christian Science high school in Greenwich, Connecticut.

In 1966, the USA was embarking upon its own cultural revolution that we three were swept up in. The civil rights movement was going strong, empowering African Americans, and the Vietnam War was kicking off, giving rise to a cultural upheaval of sorts among young white Americans. Hair was getting longer (on guys), skirts shorter (on girls), bell-bottom pants were cool and marijuana and hard drugs were lurking around every corner (at least in the imaginations of parents). Sarah Lawrence College, always a bastion of feminism and political liberalism, joined the rebellion and Mom quickly joined the revolution, having always been a liberal at heart.

Josie and I, stuck in the conservative Daycroft School, were trying our best to catch up with our studies while figuring out what it meant to be good "Americans" and "Christian Scientists" in this era of deep cultural turmoil. On the one hand, there was Grandad DeGarmo's America of baseball, electrical appliances and Godliness; on the other, the new wave of youth opposed to the "establishment" and everything it stood for. For us island kids, it was a confusing time. Mom was more at home with the changing times than we were and was making cool new college friends who would visit our apartment and chat about their sex lives and rant about social inequality, the Vietnam War and feminism.

Mom completed her BA and then a Master's in musicology at Sarah Lawrence in 1970 and started to look around for work. She found a job as the music teacher at Derryfield High School, a private preparatory school in Manchester, New Hampshire, catering to the well-to-do families keen to keep their kids from becoming drug addicts and their sons from getting drafted to go to Vietnam. The principal was Ralf Scozzafava, a man who was destined to become the "establishment" figure for the more liberal teachers, my mother included, of course, and the more rebellious (but rich) students.

Josie and I were granted free admission to Derryfield, solving the education issue for us. We were both glad to leave Daycroft behind and join a "normal" school devoid of Christian Science. But we weren't confident in our own "normalcy," with traces of Grenadian black sand still between our toes.

It was not an easy time to be an authority figure, as teachers generally are. My mother's first year was a nightmare. The snooty Derryfield students, especially the girls, were hateful to her, disrespectful, rebellious in a puerile, pampered way and refused to take music seriously. She tried to dumb down the songs with more popular tunes but the girls initially refused to participate. Finally, Ann Page, a Jehovah's Witness disciple and a scholarship case, broke the silence and joined in on one of my mother's solo efforts. That broke the back of the resistance, and eventually she became one of the more popular teachers at Derryfield, inspiring many students to become music lovers, if not musicians.

My mother was also popular among her fellow teachers, especially the more liberal ones such as Kevin Cullin, Robert Lemur, Larry Jacques, Steven Thomas and Philip Currier. These rebels would gather in 1971 at our old rented house in the woods of Reeds Ferry (now Bedford), on a dirt road, for barbeques or Indonesian *rijst tafels*, to plot against the dictatorial rule of Scozzafava (he fired most of them) and rant against the more significant mismanagement of President Richard Nixon in his duplicitous handling of the Vietnam War.

Mom, Josie and I were a team between 1970 and 1972, living out in the woods on Stowell Road. Mom had divorced my father in 1968, against his objections, forcing us to spend a summer in Idaho, which happened to have the most liberal divorce laws in the country, and one of the most illiberal populations. Herbert died shortly thereafter in 1969. There had been suitors over the years, but Mom had turned them all down. Some were frightened away by my pet Couti Mundi, my birthday present in 1970.

Philip Currier, my French teacher, went through his own divorce from his first wife Diane in the summer of 1972. He was interested in the music teacher, but Mom had made it clear that she would not get involved with him until the divorce was settled. Diane moved to Belmont, Mass, with their two children—Danielle and James. He would later gain custody of the two children after Diane had a nervous breakdown and was declared unfit.

A romance between the French teacher and music teacher started to bloom after Phil and my mother volunteered to attend a weekend drug rehabilitation workshop in Boston, Mass. "Derryfield was reeling with drugs back then," Phil said. "And part of the workshop was to create situations where the teachers had to confront themselves and their own prejudices and their own inner feelings about relationships. That was the weekend we began being together. We just realized, over the weekend that we really liked each other. I was still raw from the divorce and was not eager to jump into a relationship. Every weekend was taken up seeing the kids and fighting with Diane, so we didn't have much of a relationship that fall, except for a friendship."

Their relationship blossomed in the halls of Derryfield in the spring of 1973, becoming a subject of gossip among the students. Much to my embarrassment, my mother was having a more exciting love life than I was in high school. Philip and my mother got married in the summer of 1975, as I was heading off to St John's College. By that time, he had gained custody of his two children, Danielle and James, who had moved in to our Stowell Road homestead, providing my mother with plenty of mothering activities now that Josie and I were out of the nest, away at our respective colleges. Josie went to Alfred College in upstate New York.

Remarkably, the Stowell Road house has survived as a fixture in my mother's marriage to Phil. They stayed on as teachers at Derryfield until 1977 when they quit their jobs and spent a year in France—Phil getting a Master's in linguistics and my mother apprenticing with the legendary Madame Nadia Boulanger. They returned to New Hampshire in 1978 to find the market for teachers was saturated and themselves over-qualified, at least in the New Hampshire market. They were not willing to leave the Bedford homestead to seek teaching positions elsewhere.

Phil dropped linguistics and became a post-and-beam contractor, naming his company Promethean Builders. Mom taught private music lessons. They have stayed together at Stowell Road for almost 50 years with no more exciting flights from paradise for my mother. Phil has proved a princely caretaker for my mother in her declining years when she has suffered from dementia and other physical setbacks. My mother, always the romantic, had finally found an anchor for her own life.

"It's been a good life and I have been wonderfully blessed having Phil as a partner," my mother said in April 2019, when she was 87 and by then suffering from fairly advanced dementia.

CHAPTER 6

EPILOGUE—MEDAN REVISITED

In February 2015, I decided to pay a visit to Medan, North Sumatra. I had started to compile the family memoir and had secured permission to visit the former headquarters of the Deli Maatschappij (Company)—the fountainhead of the Janssen and Cremer families' fortunes. I felt the need to do a little journalistic-style research on modern Medan. From Bangkok I flew to Penang, Malaysia, meeting up there with a Swiss journalist friend Peter Sidler, once based in Bangkok, and from there we flew to Medan, a short hop. Sidler, retired, was interested in my family quest and decided to tag along for the ride.

I had previously visited Medan in 2003, on a *tempo dulu* tour with my mother, stepfather Philip Currier, sister Josie and her two children Tyrone and Molly and my own Asian clan, wife Suwannee, daughter Sarah and son Herbert. On that trip we had discovered our old home in Batang Kuis. By 2015, although we searched diligently for the old homestead, having hired a driver and guide, we failed to find the place. The house had apparently been torn down to make way for some new housing development. Much of the countryside around Medan, verdant just 12 years ago, had been consumed by urban sprawl, especially the fertile Polonia district which had been covered with tobacco plantations during my parents' stay in North Sumatra six decades previously between 1953 and 1957.

Medan, a swampy backwater when my ancestors chose it for the *rumah panjung* (house on stilts) that originally housed the Deli Maatschappij, is now Indonesia's fifth-most-populous city, suffering all the classic symptoms of rapid economic development—horrendous traffic, posh shopping malls juxtaposed with sprawling slums, ugly shophouse constructions along every road, ubiquitous mom & pop retail outlets on every street corner, hazardous sidewalks (who walks when you can ride a motorcycle?) and air pollution. It has come a long way from its "Paris of Sumatra" days.

And yet there were remnants from the Dutch colonial times, hidden within the havoc, thanks to the heroic efforts under way at the preservation of some historical sites, the result of endeavors by private individuals rather than the local government. The old Deli Maatschappij headquarters, for instance, was bought by a local businessman who decided to renovate the building, restoring it to its original splendor while maintaining its architectural integrity but, unfortunately, just for his personal use. It could have been worse. Another businessman who bid for the building had allegedly wanted to turn the property into an illegal casino or brothel, according to sources in Medan.

After the Indonesian army seized all the plantations and buildings belonging to Dutch companies, including the Deli Maatschappij and Senembah Maatschappij, the two tobacco companies founded by my ancestors, on December 10, 1957, the properties were first placed under military control. Later, they were shifted to management by a state company PTP (Plantations Enterprise), sub-divided into nine separate entities, set up by President Sukarno to manage nationalized Dutch plantations. Deli Company was placed under the management of PTP IX while Senembah went under the management of PTP II. Initially, the PTPs did okay, once they had removed the army from the picture.

"These army officers didn't know anything about plantations," said Soedjai Kartasamita, a former Director General of all the PTP enterprises. "They only knew about marching, so they made people on the plantations march every morning. Fortunately, the government realized it was not a good policy to have the army in charge, so that's why the Indonesian senior staff became the top officials in the plantations and they did a good job, because they were well-trained by the Dutch," Kartasamita said in an interview in 2015 when he was 89 years old.

Despite their valiant efforts, the history of the North Sumatran tobacco plantations under the PTPs was one of gradual decline after the departure of the Dutch, not necessarily due to the loss of Dutch efficiency but rather to a variety of factors including the voracious urban development around Medan, the rise of palm oil plantations as an alternative and more profitable crop, a drop off in tobacco consumption due to rising health concerns about smoking and the labor- and soil-intensive nature of the tobacco plant.

"Another reason was climate change," Kartasamita said. "There is more rain now, even during the tobacco planting season. You need only 72 days to grow tobacco, and you want rain in the afternoons, not the mornings, and not

Deli Company Building in Medan, with the statue of
Jacob Theodore Cremer in front of it.

during the harvest. And you have to rotate the crop, let the land lie fallow for three years, and the farmers thought the fallow land was vacant, so they occupied it. And PTP is a government company so it's not good for them to abuse people by pushing them off their land," he added.

After the departure of the Dutch, including my family and myself, aged one, in December 1957, the Indonesian government shifted its auctions of Sumatran tobacco from Rotterdam, Holland, to Bremen, Germany, in 1958. The auctions worked well the first couple of years, disproving the Dutch claim that Indonesians were incapable of managing the tobacco plantations themselves (some Dutch companies had set up an office in Singapore in anticipation of being recalled) but eventually the industry went into decline for the reasons cited above.

"Until 1960, the total tobacco area under cultivation was about 50,000 hectares, producing about 45,000 bales (of tobacco) a year," Kartasamita said. "From 1970–1990, the area declined to about 20,000 hectares, producing about 20,000 bales and from 2000 the area declined drastically to 5,000 hectares producing about 5,000 bales. Then it declined further from 2010 to 2,000 hectares and 1,500 bales and now it is about 200 bales a year," he told me in a follow-up interview in 2018, when I revisited Medan to work on a few feature stories.

Amid the decline of the tobacco plantations, the PTP IX and PTP II—in charge of the former Deli and Senembah plantations, respectively—also went into decline. There was a series of scandals as the state enterprises became embroiled in dubious land deals, selling the public-owned land off for golf courses and other property projects. One such scandal involved the Deli Maatschappij headquarters, located

*The author caught in a moment of reverence at the pedestal
of Jacob Theordore Cremer.*

in what is now a central district of the Medan metropolis. The building was auctioned off by PTP IX, which had used it as an office, in 2003, with two bidders contending for it, a Sino-Indonesian businessman reputedly involved in various shady activities, and Haji Anaf, a powerful businessman of Afghan descent who made his fortune in the palm oil planation sector.

"Luckily Anaf won the bid," said Soehardi Hartono, Director, Hartono Architects Company. "A fence was put around the building and it sat empty for several years." Hartono earned his architectural degree in Bandung, Java, before returning to Medan in 2002, when he joined the Sumatra Heritage Trust, a private-sector body devoted to preserving the city's historical sites.

Built in 1911, the Deli Maatschappij office replaced the modest *rumah panjung* office the company had occupied since 1869, situated near the confluence of two rivers—the Deli and Babura—used to transport tobacco of the Deli Company warehouses and take the cured tobacco in bales to ships waiting in the harbor at Belawan. By 1911, Jacob Theodore Cremer (an ancestor on my paternal grandmother's side) had already left the Deli Company and was the President (1907–1912) of the Dutch Trading Company. Although Cremer had never set foot in the Deli Maatschappij headquarters in Medan, it was his enduring aura as an astute businessman that had inspired Haji Anaf to bid on and buy the property in 2003, according to Hartono. Anaf was under the misimpression that Cremer had used the building as his private residence.

In 2007, after letting the building sit idle for four years, Anaf hired Hartono to help with the renovation of the Deli Company building in keeping with its former architectural style, described by Hartono as "neo classical." The renovation took around ten years to complete. "Structurally it was sound, but some parts of the windows or floors had been eaten by termites," said Hartono. There was nothing much left in terms of the original furniture and decorations, after PTP IX had abandoned the building. To repair a unique glass mosaic decoration in the atrium of the entrance, Hartono hired a couple in Semerang, Sumatra, who specialized in glass work. The floor tiles on the ground floor and massive balcony surrounding the first floor were replaced by a firm in Yogjakrta that has been making Dutch-style tiles since 1820. "And up to now they still produce old tiles," Hartono said.

Certain additions are new, such as the karaoke and video room on the first floor for Anaf's guests and the restrooms accompanying the four VIP bedrooms upstairs. "The restrooms are new. We couldn't find any in the old building except one in the parlor on the ground floor," Hartono said. "What is great about this building is it is an example of tropical-sensitive architecture. There are two-and-a-half to three-meter-wide balconies. This helps to cool down the building because the rooms don't get direct sunlight. A similar concept was utilized on the ground floor. Below the floorboards is 40 centimeters of space before the ground. So even nowadays when it is hot outside, because of the ventilation under the floors it comes out cooler." Unfortunately, instead of being turned into a tourist attraction for Medan, the Deli Maatschappij headquarters is now a pleasure palace for a palm oil tycoon.

"It was a mistake to sell the Deli Company Building," said Kartasamita, who is now General Chairman of the Indonesian Plantations Association. The PTP IX director responsible for selling the building was eventually tried,

Soedjai Kartasasmita, General Chairman of the Indonesian
Plantation Assocaition (IPA), 89, who was there in 1957 when
the Dutch planations were seized.

*Repainting the sign of PTP II which took over the family-founded
Senembah Company (old office in background), in Patumbale
District, Medan.*

convicted and imprisoned. "He was found guilty of not
following the right procedures to sell the property. There
were regulations because it was a government-owned
property," Kartasamita said. "It is considered to be a
heritage building."

Anaf, now the proud owner of the Deli Company Building, has added a bit of Janssen/Cremer heritage to the
compound, which covers two hectares. Right in front of
the building he has erected a statue of Jacob Theodore
Cremer, commissioned by Cremer's second son August
(my great grandfather) in 1923, to commemorate the successful capitalist, also known as "Coolie Cremer" at the
nadir of his career for his pivotal role in pushing through
the Coolie Ordinance in the Dutch Parliament. The statue
was originally erected by in front of the Medan Planters

Association, but by 1941 was sitting in front of the Deli Company as seen in a family photo. "After independence, it just disappeared and somehow it was found in the Public Works Department," Hartono said. "So, when Pak Anaf bought the building the mayor gave the statue to Pak Anaf and it was put in his office for a few years. Later we transferred it to the front of the Deli Building where it now stands."

After my Dutch ancestor Cremer returned to Holland in 1882 as a fabulously wealthy man, he bought the Duin en Kruidberg mansion in Santpoort, the Netherlands, where he had a statue of Mercury erected in the garden, demonstrating his respect for the Greek God traditionally associated with commerce and therefore worshipped by Greek and Roman merchants. Ironically, the statue of Cremer now standing outside Deli Company building is likewise there to glorify his commercial success, perhaps in the hope that it will rub off on the current owner, Mr. Anaf. One wonders whether ancestor Cremer would he be pleased with his posthumous deification.

Cremer is not the only famed merchant with a great mansion to commemorate his commercial success in modern Medan. No tour to Medan nowadays is complete without a visit to the Tjong A Fie Mansion on Jalan Kesawan—the main shopping and business drag in Medan in the Dutch days. The mansion is named, appropriately, after Tjong A Fie, a Chinese tycoon who made his fortune off the plantation economy and went on to become one of the largest landowners in Medan. He owned 23 tobacco and rubber plantations and 75% of the city real estate, two banks, hotels and shares in the Swatow Railway in Guangdong province, southern China. He is also remembered fondly as a great philanthropist, having built schools, hospitals, a Christian church, Buddhist temple and even a mosque for the local Muslim community in Medan in his lifetime.

Tjong A Fie (pronounced Cheong Ah Fee) died in 1921, just before Jacob Theodore Cremer, and his Deli Bank went bankrupt in 1922, forcing his offspring to sell several plantations in order to pay off the bank's debts i.e. repay depositors and so on. The Swatow Railway went bust during World War II. Slowly the Tjong family fortune dwindled away, with descendants forced to sell plantations and property to pay for school tuition and living expenses, until the survivors

Mimi Tjong, caretaker of the Tjong A Fie House museum in Medan, Indonesia.

decided to turn the Tjong A Fie mansion into a living museum in 2009, primarily to revive awareness of their benevolent ancestor, but also to help pay for its maintenance.

The mansion, a classic example of Malacca Straits architecture combining European, Chinese and Malay styles, is in need of a complete renovation, similar to the remake of the Blue Mansion in Penang, originally owned by a business associate of Tjong A Fie. But the likelihood of the Tjong A Fie mansion being sold to a private buyer is remote. The tycoon specified in his will that the house should never be sold, to ensure there was always a place for his descendants to live. At present, the main caretaker is Mimi Tjong, the youngest daughter of Tjong A Fie's fourth son by his third of three wives.

"My brother decided to turn the house in to a museum," Mimi Tjong told me in an interview in 2018. "My brother wanted people to remember my grandfather's name because people were starting to forget about him. That was the reason. It was not an easy decision, because some family members were against it. In the end, they realized that we should do it for my grandfather. We need to remind people of him. And there is another reason ... the maintenance cost is high," she said with a laugh. "But I want a real restoration, like the Blue Mansion, before I die," Mimi Tjong said.

Indonesians of Chinese descent in Medan are generally proud of Tjong A Fie's legacy, even though there were some shady spots along his path to wealth and power. Tjong A Fie's initial fortune was derived from acting as a middleman between the Dutch and the primarily Chinese coolies working on the plantations. My ancestor Cremer was instrumental in putting Tjong A Fie on his road to riches, according to Medan-based Dutch historian Dirk Buiskool.

Mimi Tjong, welcome to my mansion.

*Tjong A Fie mansion, an architecual combo of Malacca, Chinese
and European styles.*

Mimi Tjong sitting in front of a portrait of her grandfather,
Tjong A Fie.

Tjong A Fie mansion, once a commercial palace, now a museum.

"Tjong A Fie became the middleman for Cremer and the Dutch, to organize food and supplies for the plantations, because they needed someone to arrange it and because the Chinese had businesses in Medan already, and they had the money to bid on the tax farms, the revenue farms," Buiskool said. Those "revenue farms" included concessions to supply the coolies with opium and gambling dens for recreation, a means of further indebting them to the plantation owners. Tjong A Fie, a Hakka Chinese, was initially brought to Medan by his uncle, who was already operating several stores in the frontier town. Unlike the plantation coolies, the Tjongs had money.

During the plantocracy, as some social scientists describe the plantation economy in North Sumatra, Medan was the economic hub for corporate headquarters, banks, hotels, public services such as the post office, restaurants and social clubs. The city was divided into zones along ethnic lines, comprising the European quarter, the Chinese quarter and the "Indigenous" Quarter around the Sultan's palace where the Muslim population was concentrated. "In 1920, about 30% of the population were Chinese, only 10% Dutch and the rest were indigenous—Malay or Javanese," Buiskool said. The Chinese were subdivided into different dialect groups, with most of the plantation coolies coming from the Teochew dialect group on the Guangdong coast. The Chinese coolies, deemed too prone to labor strikes, were slowly replaced by Javanese workers on the plantations over the decades. "The Chinese coolies settled outside the city, started vegetable farms. It was a different group that moved to the city—Hokkien, Hakka and Cantonese," Buiskool said.

"Although it wasn't democratic, still they worked together to build up the city," Buiskool said, citing his own research.

"The Chinese built up the city in terms of housing and trade," he said. The Dutch historian even had some kind words for my ancestor, "Coolie Cremer", the main author of the Coolie Ordinance which allowed the plantations to impose their own penalties on labourers to keep them in line. "Cremer remains an important figure—positive and negative," Buiskool said. "He achieved a lot and he was the one who set up the structure of the plantations so they could be so profitable. But there was a price to pay." The price was in terms of workers' lives cut short by accidents and disease and laboring under inhuman conditions, at least during the first few decades.

Work conditions on the plantations had improved by the pre-World War II period and were fairly humane by 1957, when the Dutch operations were nationalized. When I visited North Sumatra in 2015, I chanced upon a Javanese man who had spent his whole life working on Sumatran plantations under first the Dutch and then the Indonesian state enterprise PTP II. I met Lasimin, 84, and his wife Mariati, 75, in Patumbale District, outside Medan. Lasimin had started his career as a tobacco plantation worker for the Senembah Company, the Janssen-run company my father had worked for. "There used to be jungle around here," Lasimin recalled. "I worked for five years under the Dutch and then they kicked all the Dutch out in 1957. I preferred the Dutch to PTP because the Dutch gave more benefits. Under PTP we got fewer benefits."

Christian Janssen, the founder of Senembah, went out of his way to ensure the company provided workers with basic medical attention and elementary schooling for their children, according to most accounts. Senembah, however, was more of an exception than the rule for the tobacco

Former tobacco worker Lasimin, 84, and his wife Mariati, 75,
in Patumbale District, outside Medan.

plantations. My uncle Wouter Nicolai, who worked for
Senembah Company between 1955 and 1957, provided
a glimpse of the plantation workers' conditions at that time,
and some of the benefits they enjoyed.

"We had many strikes and always at critical moments
such as when the seedlings needed watering four times a
day," Nicolai said. "We generally were able to hire the same
striking workers to come in to freelance. The labor contracts
were quite liberal in the benefits offered. Sundays and holidays were paid for. The women got three days menstrual
leave per month," he noted. "Maternity leave was six weeks.
The expectant mothers came back to work in the caterpillar
gather crews (not permanent employees) and worked until
the delivery of the baby, and were back to work the next
day, so quite some extra income." He said the Senembah

operated two hospitals, each with two Dutch doctors and two Dutch nurses, plus the additional Indonesian staff, and education was provided for the workers' children. "Besides payment in cash, each employee got payment in kind—rice, oil and textiles," Nicolai said.

The post-independence period saw the drastic decline in the economy after the Dutch companies were nationalized and much of Europe turned its back on Indonesia. This resulted in food and medicine shortages in the vast archipelago, followed by the fall of Sukarno and the rise of military strongman Suharto who unleashed an anti-communist crackdown that left half a million suspected communists dead. Given the horrors many Indonesians had to live through, it is not altogether surprising that some elderly people look back on the Dutch days with some fondness and forgiveness.

One such forgiver is Soedjai Kartasamita, the former Director of all the PTP enterprises, whom I had the honor of interviewing twice, first in 2015 and then again in 2018, both times in Medan. On December 10, 2017, Kartasamita presided over the opening of the Indonesian Plantations Museum (Museum Pekebunan Indonesia) in Medan, situated at the Palm Oil Institute. The museum was the result of years of tireless and unpaid effort on the part of Kartasamita and his assistants. "The museum is just to show people that in the past we did very well. We used to be an example for the rest of the world of the best plantations because of research and great management," Kartasamita said.

While the Deli region, and the Deli and Senembah tobacco companies, partly founded by my ancestors, must always carry the burden of their histories of exploitation and abuse of labor, the region's commercial roots have also left a legacy of ethnic tolerance unusual in Indonesia. This is something to be proud of and is partly attributable to the pragmatism of the Dutch in designating the area a commercial entrepot, welcoming investors and entrepreneurs from everywhere. That openness seems to have lingered on in the city, at least in terms of attitudes towards the different ethnic groups now inhabiting the metropolis. "Medan is an example of a tolerant Indonesian city," Kartasamita said. "Medan is very tolerant of people of Indian descent, Chinese origins. They are all Indonesians."

That is particularly good news for the Sino-Indonesians, who now account for about 10% of Medan's population. "When they [Indonesians] talk about preserving our diversity, difference in religion and race, most of the conversation is actually around the existence of Chinese immigrants in Indonesia, not Indians," said Hartono, himself of Chinese descent. "Even though there are Arab and Indian communities, it is the Chinese who are always in the spotlight," he said. "And that's why the conservation of the Tjong A Fie house could play an important role in addressing the issue. We should learn from the history of a figure like Tjong A Fie who tried to immerse himself into the community and to integrate himself into the community."

Soedjai Kartasasmita opened the museum on Dec 10, 2018, the anniversary of the seizure of Dutch plantations in Medan in 1957.

Indonesian Platation Museum in Medan.

APPENDIX

THE TEACHER BY COLIN WILCOX

The idea of school on a Sunday to me as a child sounded very unfair. However, my friend Peter was going, so it couldn't be too bad. But then he had to go, his mother was the Sunday School teacher. Peter and his sister Josie were the only other children for several miles. None of us went to Church, but Peter's mother, Mrs. Janssen, decided that we—well, her children anyway—needed some grounding in religious education, and when better to do that than on a Sunday. My parents were somewhat dismissive of religious views, but probably felt that there was no harm in me and my brother at least learning the basics.

Sundays always have a bit of a magical timeless feel to them, and for me as a child in the West Indies, I would wake up within the sound of, and a short dash away from, a palm tree beach, with nothing more pressing to do on Sundays than to explore the infinite potential of an undefined day.

So now comes the prospect of school on Sunday? Yet it was to be at Peter's home, and I had many positive associations with his household. Peter's sister, Josie, would be there. She was about my age, and she was the only girl I knew. They had a dog, Rex, a rough-looking brown and black mongrel, who came to his name and would fetch thrown sticks. With a little persuasion, Mrs. Janssen would serve up chocolate and cream Oreo biscuits from a package, not homemade cookies, and a large jug of purple colored, grape-flavored, Kool-Aid, items prohibited at my home. And who knows, maybe God could be fun!

Mrs. Janssen herself was rather exotic in my mind. She was American for a start. Slim with long dark hair, she was new to the Caribbean, and had been a teacher in the States. That meant that she knew how to communicate with children. She talked to me, not at me, and seemed genuine in what she said and how she listened. She was good natured, I thought. Of course she lived in a different universe, that of adults, but thinking back, she can only have been in her late twenties at the time.

We would sit in her living room, with the wide terrace doors open and the sunlit garden beckoning outside, and Mrs. Janssen would read stories and tell us tales. There was discipline, we weren't allowed to pinch each other or whisper, but I don't recall any long boring sermons, or teachings about sin and eternal damnation.

To be frank, my overriding memory of Sunday School is of Mrs. Janssen banging enthusiastically on the piano while we belt out the words to—and especially the chorus of—Onward Christian Soldiers. That was always the hymn we would request, and for the first few weeks at least Mrs. Janssen would acquiesce, but later she would try and steer us towards more holy, or at least more compassionate, hymns.

We learnt about Noah's Ark and the Good Samaritan, Sheep and Shepherds, someone called Jesus who lived a good and exalted life, and a God that watches over us in a kindly manner.

We learnt The Lord's Prayer. I memorized it until I could rattle it off "by heart" as confidently and as proudly as I could recite my 5 times table. I am not sure that I fully understood all about "trespasses" and "temptations", but it made me feel a little bit safer in this mortal world knowing that I had a great cosmic God on my side.

I had, and probably still have, a rather naive view of God. Not as any kind of white bearded man in the sky, but as a benevolent force that permeates everything, and listens, and maybe even communes back to us, through the day to day experiences of life.

I have never been keen on Church, but I do still pray. And when no other words come or I am not feeling, in that moment, particularly thankful or blessed, then I can glide along the smooth, well-worn pathway of The Lord's Prayer, without having to think about anything but the mantra of the familiar words linked together like beads.

When I think back to the origin of that prayer, what comes to mind is not Jesus, defiantly delivering his Sermon on the Mount, but Mrs. Janssen, sitting on her sofa, patiently attempting to pass on a deeper appreciation of life to four squirming children, more concerned about when we would get our Kool-Aid and biscuits and what time the low tide would most suit a swim.

ENDNOTES

1   C.L.M. Penders—The West New Guinea Debacle, University of Hawaii Press, page 264.

2   C.L.M. Penders—TWNGD, page 265.

3   David Chilosi & Giovanni Federico—Asian Globalization, Market Integration, Trade and Economic Growth, 1800–1938, London School of Economics, page 7 chart.

4   C.L.M. Penders—TWNGD, page 36. C.L.M. Penders, TWNGD, page 200. Gavin, Matt, Two to Be Remembered, Chapter 40.

5   C.L.M. Penders—TWNGD, page 22.

6   Dorothy Reed—End the Silence, Chapter 25.

7   Reuters, Washington D.C. dateline, Dec 10.

8   United Press, Jakarta dateline, Dec 11.

9   Dirk A. Busikool—The Chinese Commercial Elite of Medan.

10   United Press, The Hague, Dec 12.

11   Tengku Luckman Sinar, SIL—The History of Medan in the Olden Times, page 77.

12   Ann Laura Stoler—Capitalism and Confrontation in Sumatra's Plantation Belt, 1870-1979, page 1.

13   Tengku Luckman Sinar, SIL, THoM, page 32.

14   Jan Breman—Taming the Coolie Beast, Oxford University Press, page 32.

15   Ann Laura Stoler - Capitalism and Confrontation in Sumatra's Plantation Belt, 1870-1979.

16   Senembah Maatschappij 1889–1939, published by the Senembah Company on its 50th anniversary.

17   Senembah Maatschappij 1889–1939, published by the Senembah Company on its 50th anniversary.

18   Senembah Maatschappij 1889–1939, published by the Senembah Company on its 50th anniversary, chart on page 9.

19   TWNGD, page 384.

20   TWNGD, page 384.

21   Tengku Luckman Sinar—The History of Medan, page 34.

22   John Anderson—Mission to the East Coast of Sumatra, page 22.

23   Tengku Luckman Sinar, THoM, page 23.

24   Jan Breman—Taming the Coolie Beast, page 29.

25   Jan Breman—Taming the Coolie Beast, page 29.

26   Jan Breman—Taming the Coolie Beast, page 38.

27   Jan Breman—Taming the Coolie Beast, page 96.

28   Jan Breman—Taming the Coolie Beast, page 127.

29 Jan Breman—Taming the Coolie Beast, page 126.

30 John Anderson—MECS, page 41.

31 John Anderson—MECS Page 196.

32 Hannigan, Tim—Raffles and the British Invasion of Java. pages 152, 153.

33 Stoler, Ann Laura—Capitalism and Confrontation in Sumatra's Plantation Belt, 1870–1979. Page 17.

34 Jan Breman—Taming the Coolie Beast, page 284.

35 C.L.M. Penders, TWNGD, page 12.

36 International Directory of Company Histories, Vol. 66. St. James Press, 2004.

37 George Brizan—Grenada - Island of Conflict.

38 George Brizan—Grenada - Island of Conflict, page 27.

39 Matthew Parker—The Sugar Barons, page 378.

40 Tim Hannigan's "Raffles and the British Invasions of Java." Published in 2012. The section on Palembang starts on page 143, under the Chapter Title "Heart of Darkness."

41 George Brizan—Grenada - Island of Conflict.

BIBLIOGRAPHY

Anderson, John – Mission to the East Coast of Sumatra in 1823 (Oxford University Press, Oxford, 1971)

Brandt, Willem – De aarde van Deli (Van Hoeve, Netherlands, 1948)

Breman, Jan – Taming the Coolie Beast: Plantation Society and the Colonial Order in Southeast Asia (Oxford University Press, Oxford, 1989)

Brizan, George – Grenada - Island of Conflict: From Amerindians to Peoples' Revolution, 1498–1979 (Macmillan Caribbean, London, 1998)

Busikool, Dirk A. – The Chinese Commercial Elite of Medan, 1890-1942: The Penang Connection (JIMBRAS, Vol 82, Part 2 (2009), pp-113–129)

Chilosi, David & Federico, Giovanni – Asian Globalization, Market Integration, Trade and Economic Growth, 1800–1938 (London School of Economics, London, 2013)

Gavin, Matt – Two to Be Remembered: A Couple's Life and Survival in the Dutch East Indies (Createspace, 2013)

Hannigan, Tim – Raffles and the British Invasion of Java (Monsoon Books Pte. Ltd. Singapore, 2012)

Janssen, August Gus – Not Guilty (Do Ha Wok Publishers, Elizabeth, Colorado, USA, 1992)

Koch, Christopher J. – The Year of Living Dangerously (Vintage, New York, 1995)

Parker, Matthew – The Sugar Barons (Windmill, London, 2012)

Penders, C.L.M. – The West New Guinea Debacle (University of Hawaii Press, Honolulu, 2002)

Senembah Maatschappij 1889–1939, published by the Senembah Company on its 50th anniversary

Shorto, Russell – Amsterdam, A History of the World's Most Liberal City (Doubleday, New York, 2013)

Stoler, Ann Laura – Capitalism and Confrontation in Sumatra's Plantation Belt, 1870–1979 (Yale University Press, New Haven, 1985)

Szekely, Ladislao – Tropic Fever: The Adventures of a Planter in Sumatra (Oxford University Press, Oxford, 1980)

Tengku Luckman Sinar, SIL – The History of Medan in the Olden Times

van den Brand, Johannes – The Millions of Deli 1902

Veere Smit, Ilse Evelin and Reed, Dorothy – End the Silence (Createspace, 2011)

Made in the USA
Middletown, DE
29 January 2020

83905668R00094